One Liners
Cutting Thru the Fog

Joel Randall

WELCOME
You are everywhere in this book
Your past, present and future
Your lies and truths
Your fears and tears
Your joy and laughter
Your thoughts
Your enlightenment

THANKS
Thank you readers
Thanks to all who helped with this book
Thanks to all of you who have been
in my life.

Published by
Heartland Publishing
Joel Randall
417-935-9146
P.O. Box 402
Seymour, MO 65746
Email:
joel_o_randall@hotmail.com
or sarvis2joel@yahoo.com

Website:
www.goheartland.com

ISBN 0-9661865-3-2

Photos by
Mary Wales North
Tucson, Arizona

Typesetting and Design by
Chris Frazer
Pleasanton, Nebraska

Printed in the United States by Morris Publishing
3212 East Highway 30 • Kearney, NE 68847
1-800-650-7888

Nebraska Religious Chant
"Go Big Red"

0985
Norsemen, including Eric the Red and Leif Ericson,
set up outposts in north American.
(Eskimos, Beothubs & Micmacs).

Individual Stories
Our individual stories prove we are different
and that we are the same.

Words / Deeds
When deeds speak, words are nothing.

Advice
It is always a silly thing to give advice,
but to give good advice is absolutely fatal.
Oscar Wilde

Grass Stains
Add a few drops of household ammonia to a teaspoon of
hydrogen peroxide and rub the stain with this mixture, rinse
with water after stain is gone.

Love
Love is an expression of the willingness to create space in
which something is allowed to change.
Harry Palmer

A Blessing
The smile of a stranger.

Earth

We are part of the Earth, and the
Earth is part of us.
Seattle

Happiness

Happiness comes from working, loving and hoping.

Idealists

When they come downstairs from their ivory towers,
idealists are apt to walk straight into the gutter.
Logan Smith

Tails

Fish have vertical tails, sea mamals have horizontal tails.

Eccentric

There are a higher percentage of eccentric among the rich
& poor than among the larger working middle class.

Sexes

As the French say, there are three sexes -
men, women and clergymen.
Sydney Smith

Advantage

Every advantage has its disadvantages.

Marriage

By all means marry; if you get a good wife, you'll become
happy; if you get a bad one, you'll become a philosopher.
Socrates

Jury
A jury is a group of twelve people of average ignorance.
Herbert Spencer

A Dandy
A Dandy - more likely to put a diamond on
his pinky than on a womans.

Acorn
An acorn is a oak in a nutshell.

Nature
Nature is my truist friend, most beautiful and delightful.

Loved
If you wish to be loved,
show more of your faults than your virtues.
Baron Lytton

Ozone / Cancer
Ozone decrease, skin cancer increases.

Thinking
If you make people think they're thinking, they'll love you,
but it you really make them think, they'll hate you.
Don Marquis

Running
Zigzag to outrun a crocodile.

Vice President

I come from Indiana, the home of more first-rate
second-class men than any state in the union.
Thomas Marshall

Wife

Wife; a former sweetheart.
H.L. Mencken

Church Fear

More people would go to church more if it weren't for
the fear of becoming like preachers.

Birth

To my embarrassment I was born in bed with a lady.
Wilson Migner

A Friend

A friend is one who knows your faults yet
loves you in spite of your virtues.

Relatives

Distant relatives are the best kind, and the further the better.
Frank Hubbard

Women

When a woman is speaking to you,
listen to what she says with her eyes.
Victor Hugo

Blessings

Watching the birth of spring.

Knowledge
If a little knowledge is dangerous, where is the man
who has so much as to be out of danger?
Thomas Hupley

Originality
Originality is undetected plagiarism.
William Ingle

A Gossip
A gossip believes more than she hears.

Genius and Stupidity
The difference between genius and
stupidity is that genius has limits.

Best Information
Your intuition supplies the best information.

1096
May 3, 1096 Speyer, Germany. Eleven Jews who refused
baptism and conversion to the despised faith of Christianity
were murdered. Days later in Worms 800 Jews were murdered and buried in mass, children not murdered were re-
named, baptized and raised as Christians. In one month eight
thousand Jews were killed by the Christian blood lust. - American Holocaust

Real Love
I have fallen madly in love with life
and life has fallen madly in love with me.

Gratitude
Gratitude brings joy and laughter into our lives.

Business

My principal business is giving commercial value to
the brilliant but misdirected ideas of others.
Thomas Edison

Prayin

Lot of people would do more prayin if
they had a soft spot for their knees.

Art

Art is man's nature; nature is God's art.
Philip Bailey

Business / Crime Motto

Get the money and run.

Resolutions

The fatality of good resolutions is that
they are always too late.
Oscar Wilde

Old Cars

Why do men like old cars and not old women?

Selling Music

Their music is good enough to sell but
their selling isn't good enough to sell it.

Blessings

Many of your blessings are unclaimed.

Good Marriage

A good marriage would be between a
blind wife and a deaf husband.
Michael Montaigne

Money

I don't like money, but it quiets my nerves.
Joe Louis

Al Capone

You can get much further with a kind word and a gun
than you can with a kind word alone.

Fire

Indian make small fire and get up close,
white man make big fire and get way back.

A Gossip

A gossip puts 2 and 2 together and makes 5.

Convents

I like convents, but I wish they wouldn't
admit any women under the age of fifty.
Napoleon

Ideal Wife

Any woman who has an ideal husband

Seven Ages & Stages Of People

Spills, Drills, Thrills, Bills, Ills, Pills & Wills.

Pioneer

In my book a pioneer is a man who turned all the grass upside down, strung bob-wire over the dust that was left, poisoned the water and cut down the trees, killed the Indian who owned the land, and called it progress. If I had my way, the land here would be like God made it, and none of you sons of bitches would be here at all.
Charles Russell speaking to the Great Falls,
Montana Booster Club, 1923

1492

There is no better race or better land, they have the softest and gentlest voices in the world and they are always smiling.
Columbus

Humans

A human being is an ingenious
assembly of portable plumbing.
Christopher Morley

Toilet Paper

Eighty percent of the world's people don't use toilet paper!

Wits

Nothing sharpens the wits like promiscuous flirtation.
George Moore

Hollywood Politically Correct Movie

Jewish actors, directed & produced by blacks,
written by Hispanics, owned by Orientals.
Politically correct movie. Indians forgotten.

Listening
Usually a quiet listener outshines a brilliant talker.

Language
Kindness is the language the blind can see
and the deaf can hear.

Washington DC Lobbyist Poll
40% of DC Lobbyists are women
60% of DC Lobbyists are men
70% of the successful DC Lobbyists are beautiful women

Camels
A camel can drink 25 gallons of water in 30 minutes.

Bad Things Happen
Sometimes bad things happen
so worse things can't happen.

A Penny
Long ago a penny saved was a penny earned.
Today a penny saved is worthless.

Fantasy - Reality
The gift of a #1 fantasy can change to a #2 reality.

Newspaper Truths
Sometimes there's more truth in the comics
than on the front page.

Bad Love Affair
The love affair was so bad that
the breaking up was the best part.

Book Business
20% of the books make 80% of the money.

Writers Discover
Most writers discover that writing
is easier than selling their work.

Abilities
The distance between abilities and lies can be short.

Nebraska Small Towns
Another advantage of rural Nebraska small towns is that
you can J walk as a pedestrian and make J turns as a
driver and probably won't get in any trouble.

How To Save Money
Do without what others spend their money for.

Repulsive Humans
Humans are even repulsive to each other. The proof is:
The close their eyes when they kiss each other.

Relative Problem
Being related to people you can't relate to.

Male Chauvinist Perception Of A Good Marriage

My wife and I do exactly as I want to.

Work

Work towards peace of mind and receive some free happiness which money can't buy.

Isolation

Isolating oneself is a chief cause of unhappiness.

Stirring

She came to me immediately stirring my life into comfortable chaos.

Busy

Too busy to enjoy life and happiness.

Weddings

The bride's family pays for the wedding so why does she take the name of her in-laws who don't pay?

Grey Whale

A grey whale weights about one ton per foot.

Creating Babies

Men experience some of the pleasure. Women then have 9 months of discomfort then experience intense pain in birthing the baby.

Beef Fat

White means grain fed, yellow means grass fed.

Deer Dropping

Deer dropping stay black, moist & glossy for 15-30 minutes.

Auto Plates

10 out of 20 auto plates on the road will be instate.

World's Largest Goose

The world's largest goose is located near Sumner, Mo.

Judge Roy Bean

"Bruno method of sobering up drunks." the drunk was chained to a post in front of the place. Bruno was chained to the same post with a slightly shorter chain. Bruno was a big bear.

Bend In The Road

Don't mistake a bend in the road for the end of the road.

Purpose

Man's purpose is to give women hell. Women's purpose is to give men hell. Mission accomplished! What's next?

Pipe Size

Double the size of a pipe and quadruple the flow.

Better Than

It was better than anything I could say about it.

1492

The American Holocaust begins. Disease, slavery, torturing, raping, killing and destruction of Native American's everything.

Born Again

Born again, thinking they got a handle on it all, but they're still wet behind the ears.

Birds

The American Robin is a thrush.

Angel

Her name was Angel because she was up in the air all day and harped all nite.

Federal Study

Recent federal study finds link between sex and pregnancy.

About Half Don't

About half of Americans don't live further than fifty miles from their childhood homes.

Newspaper Headline

If strike isn't settled quickly, it may last a while.

Electrolux Ad

"Nothing sucks like Electrolux" ad pulled after 2 days.

President John Tyler

Only president to elope while in office.

Nova

The Chevy Nova sold poorly in south America.
GM changed the name to "Caribe" when
learned that "Nova" means it won't go.

Columbus Letter Excerpt

After searching the coasts of all the islands for wealth
and great cities we sent two men up country. They traveled
for three days and found an infinite number of small
villages and people without number,
but nothing of importance.
Columbus

Abused Children

Abused children are more addictive as adults.

Merging Language

Merging, language disappearing,
into the silence, of seeing & knowing.

Government & God

In God we trust, all others, we monitor.

Success

She's the kind of girl who climbed the ladder
of success, wrong by wrong.
Mae West

Texas

General Sheriden said "If I owned Texas and Hell,
I would rent Texas and live in Hell."

Love
Love comes in many shades and degrees.

Desire
Dante's breathless feeling for Beatrice described as
"The desire of the moth for the star" ends up being
"the moth drawn into the flames."

Criticism
All this criticism, is like ducks off my back.
Samuel Goldwyn

Giving
The way you give is more important than what you give.

Pintos
Pintos sold poorly in Brazil. Ford learned that
pinto was slang for "tiny male genitals".

Bobby
I don't see what's wrong with giving Bobby a little
experience before he starts to practice law.
John F. Kennedy, after appointing his brother
Attorney General

Old West Macho Man
Outdrinking, Outfighting, Outcussing, Outguessing.

Common Sense
His lack of common sense couldn't be blamed on higher
education because he didn't have any common sense
before the higher education either.

Auto AC

The first automobile to offer air conditioning
was Packard in 1939.

One Room Country School

He attended a one room country school & learned
the three R's (Readin, Ratin, & Rithmetic).
He learnt all 25 letters of the alphabet too.

Efficient Government

Whenever you have an efficient government,
you have a dictatorship.
Harry Truman

Principles

The best principles if pushed to excess,
degenerate into fatal vices.
Archibald Alison - 18th Century Scottish Clergyman

Learning

We learn to do most things by making a fool of ourselves,
then hanging in there for some more rounds.

1512

Spanish law gives Spanish land grantees the right to make
slaves of Indians under the encomienda system.

Names

Goody P. Creep, operates a funeral home.

Laziest
The laziest person will find the
easiest way to do something.

Her Ex
Her ex was the inspiration for a Halloween mask.

Light Bulb
In developing the light bulb Edison discovered
over 50,000 things that didn't work.

You're County If
You're country if there's Bag Balm in the medicine cabinet.

Bronze Star
The United States Army issued the Bronz Star
to seven soldiers for firing (mistakenly) on stranded
US troops during the Persian Gulf War.
Chuck Shepherd - News of the Weird

Super Bowl
NFL sponsored Super Bowl events generated 313 tons
of trash in January 1995.

Adversity
Adversity makes a man wise, not rich.

Granddaughter Perception
A five year old cute granddaughter visiting the ranch
thought all the cows were for sale cause they had
price tags in their ears.

Cartoons

About 90% of the US TV cartoon
programs are drawn in Asia.

Potosi Bolivia Silver Mine

1544 began the silver mining that cost
8 million indigenous lives.

When Women Go Wrong

When women go wrong, men go right after them.
Mae West

Accidents

Accidents are more likely near schools, hospitals,
theatres and nursing homes.

Farmers

1910 farmers got 40% of the retail price of food.
1992 farmers got 9% of the retail price of food.

Corn

About half of it is fed to livestock.

Buying A Bad Story

I was young and I thought I was tough and I knew it was
beautiful and I was a little bit crazy but hadn't noticed it yet.
Norman Maclean

Answers

Seek the truth, study, ask the Elders.

What A Deal

Fall of 98 - Russians made a deal to receive 1.5 million tons of free wheat from the U.S.A., the Russians will continue to sell their own wheat abroad.

Repeal Helmet Laws

Repeal all cycle helmet laws,
we need more organ donors.

Bushel Of Corn

A 56# bushel of corn makes 32# starch or 33# corn syrup.

Ignorant

You are ignorant if you don't know how very little we know.

Spiritual Arrogance

Any person of any faith who believes they have all the truth has a problem with spiritual arrogance.

Love

Love is knowing you are no better than others.

What Is

There is no beginning, there is no end.

Hell On Wheels

First used to describe the tent towns which kept even with the end of the railroad tracks as they moved westward.

Western

The only western to win the Academy Award for Best Picture was "Cimarron" in 1931.

President

Mothers want their sons to grow up to be president, but they don't want them to become politicians in the process!
John F. Kennedy

Advice

Rosalind Russell once sat down next to a man who had a terrible cold. She advised him to drink lots of fluids, take two aspirin, go to bed right now and you'll feel better in the morning. The man was obviously unimpressed and looked at her with mild annoyance. She quickly introduced herself as Rosalind Russell and said "I make movies". The man said "I'm Charles Mayo and I run a medical clinic."

Love Consummated

Our love was consummated into her marriage to another.

Accurate Answer

Need an accurate answer?
Just go back another ten thousand years.

Day / Nite

Day escapes into nite, nite escapes into day.

Politicians Promise

Politicians promise more security
and then you are sacrificed.

Love

Don't love out of fear, Don't fear to love.

France

If there were anything I could take back to France with me,
It would be Mrs. Kennedy.
Charles de Gaulle

Elephants

The circumference of an elephants front foot equals it's
shoulder height from the ground.

Diapers

Minimum diapers - one every 2 hours.

Bra Test

Ann Landers bra test - place a pencil under your breast,
if it falls to the floor you don't need to wear a bra.

Lovers

Latex lovers live longer.

1584

On Virginia Indians, a more kind and loving
people can not be found in the world.
Arthur Barlowe

Sales Tip

Blue covers sell better than green on science fiction books.

Poets

Poets utter great and wise things which they
do not themselves understand.
Plato

Life
The longer you've lived the sooner your gonna die.

Tires
Minium tire tread penny measurement
is to the top of Lincoln's head.

Balance
Pessimists usually live with optimists.

Bodies
The distance from your elbow to your wrist
is also the length of your foot.

Strangers 1633
Since you are here as strangers, you should rather
confine yourselves to the customs of our country
than impose yours upon us.
Wicomesse Leader

Water Use
29 gallons to produce a pound of tomatoes, 139 gallons to
produce a pound of bread, 2,464 to produce a pound of beef.

Too Many
Too many have strayed from the path
shown by the Great Spirit.
Sequichie Grandfather

Rain
When there is a ring around the moon, the number of
stars inside the circle equal the number of days till it rains.

Fashion

Current fashion is fickle, seldom lasting more than 2 years.

Age

Age is not a particularly interesting subject. Anyone can get old. All you have to do is live long enough.
Groucho Marx

Hitchhiker Sign

Anywhere but here.

Size

Your wedding ring & hat size are the same.

Land Movement

This continent is moving north at about the rate your fingernails grow.

Experience

People pretty much experience what they believe – even though sometimes they don't believe they believe it.
Harry Palmer

Heat

A pound of coal gives double the heat of a pound of wood.

Mice

When you see a mouse in your house there are probably 6-12 you didn't see.

Electricity

On pound of coal makes one kilowatt hour of electricity.

Actions

Actions speak louder than words,
but unfortunately not as often.

Negative

Negative questions get negative answers.

Food

One quart of dried beans will feed a dozen people.

Age and Youth

There is nothing more certain than that age and youth are
right, except perhaps that both are wrong.
Robert Louis Stevenson

Height

Your height at 22 months times 2 will be your adult height.

Sex

The only unnatural sex act is that
which you cannot perform.
Alfred Kinsey

Flowers

Honeybees prefer blue flowers over red flowers.

Acting

The most import thing in acting is honesty. Once you've
learned to fake that, you're in.
Samuel Goldwyn

Banking
Each bank teller loses about $250 a year.

Late 1630's
In the Massachusetts Bay Colony it became illegal to
shoot a gun for any reason except to kill an Indian or a wolf.

Popcorn
A cup of popcorn makes 30-40 cups of popped popcorn.

Weight
Double you height in inches
for your ideal weight in pounds.

Bites
Most bites are done by females of the species.

Sex Talk
Talk between lovers about techniques to improve sex
is destructive in bed and constructive out of bed.
Theodore Isaac Rubin

Mother Nature
You can't improve on Mother Nature.

Affluent Residential
The more affluent residential areas are usually on
the north and west part of a city.

Civil War
Civil War battles - 150# of lead per soldier killed.

Woman

A woman is her mother.
Anne Sexton

Best Opening Line

The best opening line is "hello".

Power

Power is the ultimate aphrodisiac.
Henry Kissinger

Weight / Measure

A pint's a pound, the world around.

Cost Of Living

I think some folks are foolish to pay what it costs to live.
Frank Hubbard

Windchill

Windchill is about the temperature minus wind speed.

1778

First treaty broken between the United States and an Indian
Nation. The Delaware Treaty broken by US whites.

Poison Ivy

Leafs of three, let it be.

Thank God

I'd like to thank God,
because she makes everything possible.
Helen Reddy, accepting her Grammy Award

Buy Direct Advice
Buy direct from farmers, artists and others whenever possible.

Policeman
I have never seen a situation so dismal
that a policeman couldn't make it worse.
Brendan Behan

Late 1600's
I do not know what is going to happen in Mexico
once the Indians are exterminated except
the Spaniards will rob & kill each other.
Geronimo de Mendieta

Age
Forty is the old age of youth, fifty is the youth of old age.
Victor Hugo

Penny Measure
4500 pennies to the gallon.

Arizona Heat
The other extreme is snow in the mountains of Arizona.
One winter it snowed 400 inches in the
white mountains of Eastern Arizona.

Inventions
Less than 1% of patented inventions
make any money for the inventor.

Acting Stupid
Most people don't act stupid; it's the real thing.

High School Students

High school students are the largest oppressed
minority in America.
Jerry Rubin

Tests

On bureaucratic multiple choice tests the
longest answer is usually the right one.

Gate Rule

Always leave a gate the way you found it.

Day To Nite

Day becomes nite when you can't tell
a black thread from a white one.

War

Vietnam, the longest war in U.S. history.
Once more they forget the Indians.

Milk

One gallon of milk makes one pound of cottage cheese.

Flag

If you want a symbolic gesture, don't burn the flag, wash it.
Norman Thomas

Youth

Youth are full of revolt and are revolting.

Steel

A cubic foot of steel weighs about 500 pounds

Thinking Illusions
A great many people think they are thinking
when they are really rearranging their prejudices.
Edward R. Murrow

Homeless
No place to go to, No place to go back to.

Black
Black is beautiful.

Blessed
Blessed, are those who listen, when no one is left to speak.
Linda Hogan

Better Residential Areas
Better residential areas are upwind from the big stinks.

Beans & Soup
Beans & soup are best on the third day.

USA
The whole country is one vast insane asylum and
they're letting the worst patients run the place.
Robert Welch

Advice
Love and live, freely, fully and lightly.

Laughter
Laughter is the shortest distance between two people.
Victor Borge

Boredom

One can be loved until boredom becomes
a mystical experience.
Logan Smith

Adventure

Your best adventure story probably wasn't fun at the time.

Trust

I never trust a man unless I've got his pecker in my pocket.
Lyndon Baines Johnson.

Action

Do every act as if it were your last.

Life

In life you throw a ball. You hope it will reach a wall and
bounce back so you can throw it again, you hope your
friends will provide that wall,
Pablo Picasso

Be

Be punctual.

Ultimate Mystery

The ultimate mystery is one's own self.
Sammy Davis Jr.

Flip Wilson

What you see is what you get.

Beating Around The Bush

You're very foolish if you try to beat around the bush - you just meet yourself coming around the bush the other way.
Betty Ford

Black / White

I want to be the white man's brother,
but not his brother-in-law.
Martin Luther King Jr.

Showing Up

Showing up is 80 percent of life.
Woody Allen

Fast Acting Relief

For fast acting relief, try slowing down.
Lily Tomlin

Humor

Where humor is concerned, there are no standards - no one can say what is good or bad, although you can be sure that everyone will.
John Kenneth Galbraith

Actions

Actions speak louder than words.

Lies

There are three kinds of lies -
lies, damned lies and statistics.
Mark Twain

Children

You have 'em; I'll amuse 'em.
Dr. Seuss

1778-1871

US Senate approves 372 treaties with Indian nations.
All broken by US whites.

Actions

Some actions are so special they have no purpose.

President James Madison

Only president to weigh less than his I.Q.

Oscar Awards

Spencer Tracy's first Oscar was made out to Dick Tracy.

Cats

The only good cat is a stir-fried cat

Mice

250 mice to a gallon.

Hell

I never did give anybody hell, I just told the truth,
and they though it was hell.
Harry Truman

McDonalds

8,500 Mcdonalds have sold over 85 billion hamburgers.

Actors / Actresses

Show me a great actor and I'll show you a lousy husband;
show me a great actress and you've seen the devil.
W.C. Fields

Why Did God Put Men On Earth?

Because a vibrator can't mow the lawn.

Medical School Nutrition

Out of 127 U.S. medical schools, 102 don't offer even 1
nutrition course.

Additions

Addictions kill, I don't want to die from your addictions, if it's
gonna be from addiction, I'd prefer it be mine not yours.

Blood

In the blood is truth.

Nationalism

Nationalism is a silly cock crowing on his own dunghill.
Richard Aldington

Wisdom

Wisdom is never marrying.

Turning To God

After the devil leaves them due to aging, people turn to god.

Prayer

Give me chastity and self-restraint --- but not yet.
Saint Augustine

Rope

Don't throw both ends of the rope to a drowning man.

My Brain

My brain: it's my second favorite organ.
Woody Allen

Love

Love makes it possible to get away from yourself.

Bore

A Bore: Someone too busy talking to listen to you.

Cabbage

A cabbage is a vegetable about the size of a
human head and containing more wisdom.

Philosopher

A philosopher is one who investigates his own insanity.

Mental Health

One of four people in this country is mentally
unbalanced. Think of your three closest friends,
if they seem okay, then you're the one.
Ann Landers

Chip

A chip on the shoulder means wood up above.

Crisis

Your fortune cookie contradicting your horoscope.

Banks
Banks, no deposit, no return.

Born Executive
A born executive is one whose parents own the business.

Holy Book
A televangelist's holy book is, a checkbook.

Skill
Pickpockets remove your wallet with the skill of a surgeon -
- but don't make as much money.

Heaven
Everybody wants to go to heaven but nobody wants to die.

Truthful Politicians
Politicians tell the truth only when
calling another politician a liar.

Blessings
Friendships that last forever.

Addictions
Your addictions reduce your freedom.

Whales
Whales are the fastest growing animals in the world.

Hotels and Women

Seventy percent of people who lock themselves
out of their rooms are women.

Burglary

Burglars hit the master bedroom first.

Prettiest Women

The prettiest women make the worse coffee.

1779

George Washington instructed Major John Sullivan to
attack the Iroguols and "lay waste all the settlements
around... that the country may not be merely overrun
but destroyed." The Irognois, the Seneca, the Mohawk,
the Onondoga, and the Caynga towns were all destroyed.
George Washington's Indian name became "Town Destroyer."

City Or Town?

US census over 2,500 It's a city under it's a town.

Benjamin Franklin

Benjamin Franklin had about 24 illegitimate children.

Words

Eskimos have more than 200 words for snow.
Italians have more than 500 words for macaroni.

Rice Paper

No rice in rice paper.

Zip Codes
20252 Smokey The Bear

Seat Belts
The 1950 Nash Rambler was the first car to offer seatbelts.

Government Land
The government collects rent on half of the land and
taxes on the other half, comes out about the same.

Quills
A porcupine can have 35,000 quills.

Salty Water
The Atlantic Ocean is saltier than the Pacific.

Round Or Flat
President Andrew Jackson wasn't sure if Earth
was round or flat, president Bill Clinton
isn't sure if womens stomachs are round or flat.

Weekend Money
Almost 50% of bank robberies are on Friday.

Blondes
Mosquitos also prefer blondes.

M & M's
Americans spend $87,000 a day on plain M & M's.

Addictions

Addictions practiced, addictions switched, addictions denied.

Richest

The richest country is Lichtenstein.

Red Paint

Red usta be the cheapest color to paint with,
now it is the most expensive.

Teeth

Toads don't, Frogs do.

Shoplifting

Shoplifters lift about 2 billion dollars worth a year.

Napoleon

Napoleon was afraid of cats.

Temporary Income Tax

In 1913, income tax on $4,000 was a penny.

Flies

A fly's taste buds are in it's feet.

Addictive Society Program

In this addictive, violent society everyone could benefit
from working a twelve - step program.

4/5's Hot

Four out of five hottest cities in USA are in Florida.

Divorce / Marriage
Three quarters of female divorcees remarry.

Purring
Cats and Brahma Bulls purr.

Tree Milk
Venezuelan cow tree's sap looks,
feels and tastes like cow's milk.

Poison Test
Cleopatra tested her poisons first on her slaves.

Present
Not being present is abusive to others and yourself.

Body Cells
About 10 trillion cells per person.

Baptism
With soap baptism is a good thing.
William Ingle

Heart
My heart goes where the wild goose goes, And my heart
knows what the wild goose knows. Wild goose, brother
goose, which is best, a ramblin soul, or a heart at rest?
Country Song

Hard Times
Hard times, can be cheap, but, not easy.

Antique Business
The antique business has been so good
that the manufacturers just can't keep up.

Breathing
Horses can't breathe through their mouths.

1782
Christian Delaware Indians are massacred by Americans.

First Billionaire
Henry Ford was Americas first billionaire.

Reading Challenge
About 14,000 years to read all the books in the Library of
Congress.

Variable Speed Of Sound
Sound travels 5 times faster in water than in air.

Eggs
Four hours to hard boil an ostrich egg.

Oxygen
Seventy percent is produced by marine plants.

Fired
Eighty percent of Americans experience
getting fired in a lifetime.

English King
King George the 1st of England couldn't speak English, he spoke German.

Backbones
A camels' backbone is as straight as a horses' backbone.

Food Poisoning
Estimated that 95% are never reported.

Seawater
About a quarter pound of salt to a gallon.

Kissing Ban
Kissing was banned in England in 1439 to prevent the spread of disease.

Bricks
The Empire State Building contains ten million bricks.

Money Pictures
Twenty percent of Americans can't tell you who's picture is on a one dollar bill.

Smartest Dogs
Border Collies are the smartest dogs.

Soda Pop
In 1900 an average American drank a dozen soda pops a year, today nearly six hundred a year.

Nostrils
Pelicans don't have nostrils.

Lincoln / Booth
John Wilkes Booth's brother saved
the life of Abe Lincoln's son.

Christians
If only all Christians could be converted to Christianity.

Teenagers
Teenagers get along better with mothers than fathers.

Extremes
From one extreme to another,
for so long, that now, moderation seems extreme.

Cherry
Cherry is the most popular sno-cone & popsicle flavor.

Admiration
We love those who admire us, but not those we admire.

Doctor Translation
We have some good news and some bad news,
translates to the good news is, I'm buying a new BMW,
the bad news is, you're going to pay for it.

Billy The Kid
Billy The Kid was buried in a shirt five sizes too big.

Hobby Dollars
200 million dollars a year on model railroads.

Beethoven
For inspiration Beethoven poured water over himself.

Ding - Dong
Ding - Dong is a real town in Texas.

Life
The whole of my life has passed like a razor,
in hot water or in a scrape.
Sydney Smith

Rain Forests
Since 1960 over 25% of the rain forests of Central & South
America have been cut down.

Classified Wedding Ad
New wedding dress, never worn, best cash
offer or trade for 38 Special.

Jell-O
Chocolate flavored Jell-O was a failure.

Candy
Americans eat more than 20 pounds
of candy a year per person.

1802
Federal law prohibits the sale of liquor to Indians.

Civil War Movies
Gone With The Wind is the only civil war movie
with no battle scene.

Growth
Fingernails grow about four times faster than toenails.

Sex At Work
About half of US workers claim having sex at work.

Death / Birth
Why is it we rejoice at a birth and grieve at a funeral?
Is it because we are not the person involved?
Mark Twain

Jumping Mammals
All mammals except the elephant can jump.

Public Bathrooms
Men's bathrooms are cleaner than women's bathrooms.

Coonskin Caps
Daniel Boone detested coonskin caps.

Keeping Children At Home
The best way to keep children at home is to make the
home atmosphere pleasant and let the air out of the tires.
Dorothy Parker

Heights
Wilt Chamberlain 7'1", his parents 5'8".

Hamburger Declaration Of Independence

The house where Jefferson wrote most of the Declaration of Independence was replaced with a hamburger stand.

Children

I like children, if they're properly cooked.
W.C. Fields

Honor

Whites achieve honor accumulating possessions
Indians achieve honor giving away possessions.

Dogs

Retrievers bite the least.

Happiness / Marriage

A woman marries to make two people happy,
herself and her mother.

Admiration

Spent a lot of time admiring his reflection.

Life

Life is, but a movement of shadow,
running across the Earth, disappearing into the sunset.

Eggs

You have to break some eggs to make an omelet.

Government Research

$277,000 on pickles in 1993.

The Difference Between A Cat And A Lie

The principle difference between a cat and a lie
is that a cat only has 9 lives.
Mark Twain

Waxed Paper

Waxed paper was invented by Thomas Edison.

Adultery

Adultery: democracy applied to love.
H. L. Mencken

Adulthood

Adulthood is a depressing destination, as you grow up,
you become adulterated.
C. W. Metcalf

Cow Leading

Easy to lead a cow upstairs hard to lead a cow downstairs.

Brains

Humans are about 2% brains.

Lotsa Eggs

American hens lay enough eggs per year
to circle the equator a 100 times.

Crying

You can't cry out in space, crying requires gravity.

Marriage
Marriage is a great institution,
but I'm not ready for an institution yet.
Mae West

Adult Education
The best adult education is children.

Yes, There Is
Yes, there is a Santa Claus, and an Easter Bunny,
and a Tooth Fairy, and yes, there are smart Cowboys.

Anger
The most angry are the most wrong.

Reality
Martin Luther King said "I have a dream."
But we Indians didn't have a dream. We had a reality.
Ben Black Elk

Adversity
Adversity reminds men of religion.
Livy

Advertising
Ads get better response near the front.

Advice
A good scare is worth more to a man than good advice.
Edgar Howe

Aeschylus Death

Aeschylus the father of Greek Tragedies died from a eagle dropping a tortoise on his head.

Afraid

Don't be afraid to be afraid.

1806

US office of Superintendent of Indian trade is established to administer federal Indian trading houses.

Alcohol

Alcohol makes married men see double and feel single.

Age

When a man gets too old to set a bad example, he starts to give good advice.

Aging Lists Growing

1. Things can't do. 2. Things don't wanna do.

Almost

One more drink and I'd have been under the host.
Dorothy Parker

Agnostic

I am an agnostic: I do not pretend to know what many ignorant men are sure of.
Clarence Darrow

Agreeable

An agreeable person agrees with me.

Al Capone

Capone's business card said
he was a used furniture dealer.

Content

We were content to let things remain as
the Great Spirit made them.
Chief Joseph

Three Wise Women

Would have arrived ahead of time, cleaned the stable,
helped deliver the baby, brought practical gifts,
and there would be peace on Earth.

Judging

Judging foolishly by income and/or possessions.

Water

One drop of water is as complete
in itself as the ocean.

Wisdom

Wisdom is knowing what to do with what you know.

God Made Man

God made man stronger but not necessarily more
intelligent. He gave women intuition and femininity.
And, used properly, that combination easily
jumbles the brain of any man I've ever met.
Farrah Faucett Majors

Alligator

Alligator eyes apart in inches are it's length in feet.

Ambition

An ambitious man can never know peace.
J. Krishnamurti

Superbowl Aftermath

Each year the country's worst spousal abuse follows the
Superbowl by four hours.
Kenneth Lincoln "Men Down West"

Brains

People have just enough brains
to tan their hides, same as the rest of the animals

All

We're all in this alone.
Lily Tomlin

America

The business of America is business.
Calvin Coolidge

Amusements

What a pity it is that we have no amusements
in England but vice and religion.
Sydney Smith

Experience

Whatever you create, you will eventually experience.
What goes around, comes around.
Harry Palmer

1808

American Fur company is chartered by John Jacob Astor to compete with Canadian fur trade.

A Prayer

Appropriately used, the power from
and of prayer can do anything.

Anger

Anger makes one speak too loud and blind.

Bob

My brother Bob doesn't want to be in government -
he promised Dad he'd go straight.
John F. Kennedy

Animals / People

Animals act like nature intended. Only man acts like a fool.

Annoying

To anyone annoying you, suggest they go sit on a pumpkin.

Antique Buyers

Big buyers of antiques come after lunch.
Lillian Hellman

Ants / Rain

Ants cover their hole before a rain.

Committee

A committee spends a lot of time doing a
poor job of something that one person could
have done a good job of in a short time.

Apex of Creation

People are not the apex of creation, just the ex-ape.

Appearance

Nothing is as it appears.

Apples

Apple juice, three gallons per bushel of apples.

Culture

The problem with blending the Indian and
European cultures is that the Indians are
devoted to living and the Europeans to getting.
John Ross McIntosh

Names

Lawless & Lynch, Law Firm, Jamaica, New York.

Arizonians

Arizonans outside the Phoenix area are grateful that one
half the states population live in the Phoenix area.

Facts

Get your facts first, and then you can
distort them as much as you please.
Mark Twain

What Is ,Is

Only your beliefs & opinions of it differ.

Free

I'm free, but, it'll cost ya!

Clubs

Please accept my resignation. I don't want to belong
to any club that will accept me as a member.
Grocho Marx

Love

Love sought is good, but given unsought is better.
Shakespeare

A Gossip

A gossip has a good sense of rumor.

Having Children

First: Having children. Second: raising children.
Third: Getting rid of them. Fourth: Make peace with them.

Art

What garlic is to salad, insanity is to art.
Saint Augustine

Phoenix Described

Phoenix Arizona: Summer all winter and Hell all summer.

The Real Reason Cowboys & Ranchers Get Married

To have someone to open the gates

Art of Government

The art of government consists of taking as much money from everyone possible and using 90% of it themselves and giving 10% to those most undeserving.

As You Are

Accept yourself as you are and then become what you can.

1824

U.S. Bureau of Indian Affairs (BIA)
is created as part of the War Department.

Progress

Progress is made by those too lazy to
do it the old hard way.

Law

Customs may not be as wise as laws,
but they are always more popular.
Disraeli

Attitudes

Attitudes can be improved by taking action.

Augustine

Early church work "The City of God" by Augustine, the
conclusion: someone who worships within the fold of
Christianity certainty is rational and human, though there
clearly are races that in some respects might
seem human, but are not.
"America Holocaust" page 168

Auto Electrical Problems

Over half of auto electrical problems involve grounding.

Average Depth

A man drowned trying to walk across a lake
with an average depth of two feet.

Awakening

Awake and be joyful and grateful every morning.

Back Pain

If your back hurts more when you climb stairs
and hills do extension exercises.

Eternity

Eternity is now, so is love.

Bad / Hot Jokes

Two bad jokes followed by a hot joke: Los Angeles smog,
New York mugging and Arizona dry heat.

Be Thankful

Be thankful for your guardian angels.

Wise

The wise are not always silent,
but they know when to be silent.

Bathing

Louis XIV bathed once a year.

Beautiful Words

The two most beautiful words in the
English language are "Check Enclosed."

Best

Make the best you can of every situation.

Men

He's the kind of man a woman
would have to marry to get rid of.
Mae West

Better Teenagers

Teenagers are better after some recycling.

Humor

Humor is just another defense against the universe.
Mel Brooks

Earth Angel

She was an earth angel, her mother was a
heavenly angel bred by the devil.

Ashes

To us the ashes of our ancestors are sacred.
Seattle

Bible Thumpers

The Bible is the most shoplifted book in the U.S.A.

Bicycling

You're geared right on your bicycle if your
lungs & legs tire at the same time.

Books

Lend only books you don't want back.

Big Fast Fact

In 1989 a 50 million ton asteroid missed hitting the
Earth by only six hours. Had the collision happened
the explosion would have exceeded the detonation
of all the worlds nuclear weapons.

Brains

Modern man's brain is smaller than Neanderthals brain.

Hate

Heaven has no rage like love turned
to hate nor hell a fury like a woman scorned.
Congreve

Borrowing

Return anything you borrow in a timely fashion.

Bilingual

American men are bilingual,
they speak English and Profanity.

Birds

Smaller birds will let you get closer to them than big birds.

Body

Your body is your temple.

Boelus Nebraska

Boelus Nebraska railroad station
is the only one to never have electricity.

Life

Life is a process of getting used to the surprises.

Law

The law, in its majestic equality, forbids the rich
as the poor to sleep under bridges,
to beg in the streets, and to steal bread.
Anatole France

Biased

Be aware that everyone is biased.

Conference Advice

Attend the business meeting and the rest
of the conference will seem better.

Men

A man in the house is worth two in the street.
Mae West

Buffalo

Buffalo won't eat alfalfa, brome grass and
non native plants if they have a choice.

Bumper Sticker

Driver carries only $20, in ammo.

Taxes And Honesty

Everybody tries to cheat successfully
on their taxes without really lying.

Common Sense

It ain't as common as it usta be.

Business Sales

Small business usually sell for 7 to 10 times the average
yearly profit of the last 3 years.

Three Serves

Those that serve, those who are served and those who
observe.

Religious Orders

Religious orders have enough religion
to war against each other.

Butter
All is not butter that comes from a cow.

Political Law
It is illegal for a politician not to smile at any
of the local citizens in Las Animos, Colorado.

Buy
Buy at every kids stand.

1830
Indian Removal Act passed by US Congress, Relocation of
Eastern Tribes to an Indian territory west of the Mississippi.

Chasing Fame
Chasing fame and fortune, forgetting
the love of simple and gentle things.

Crazy Horse
Crazy Horse didn't drink.

War
Either war is obsolete or man is.
Buckminster Fuller

Education / Experience
Education is what you get from reading the small print in a
contract. Experience is what you get from not reading it.

Ordinary
Ordinary is sacred

Flat Tire

When a normal person has a flat tire, they call triple A.
When an alcoholic has a flat tire,
they call the suicide hotline.

Government

There is no government like no government.

Greeting Card Writing Opportunity

Needed: Easy-to-read
Graduation cards.

Guilty

Guilty until proven wealthy.

Heart

I am opening my heart to speak to you ---
open yours to receive my words.
Como

Victory / Massacre

When a white army battles Indians and wins,
it is called a great victory, but if they
lose it is called a massacre.
Chicksika, Shawnee

John Wayne

John Wayne was a collector of dolls.

Weight

Over 50 % of Americans would like to lose weight.

Osceola 1838

They could not capture me except under a white flag.
They cannot hold me except with a chain.
Osceola Seminole

Mother-in-Laws

Most men like their wives' mother.
Most women don't like their husbands' mother.

Honesty

Honesty is not an equitable policy.
Alexander the Great

Life

Life is between before birth and after death.
Or, life is after birth and before death.

Love and Pain

To love is sometimes painful, not to love is more painful.

Neighbor Said

Our neighbor said: I'm Dutch and German and
neither amount to much.

Milk

Don't cry over spilt milk.
There's already enough water in it.

Nature of Things

Life consuming life. It is the nature of things;
creation, as created.

Humor
Nothing is quite as funny as the unintended humor of
reality.
Steve Allen

Nostalgia
Nostalgia is one more thing that gets better with age.

Politically Correct Politician
More liberal than any democrat
More conservative than any republican

Thoughts
Your thoughts shape your future.

Professional Writer
It took me 15 years to discover that I had no talent
for writing, but I couldn't give it up because
by then I was too famous.
Robert Benchley

Promises
I have been trying to seize the promises
which they made me -- but I cannot find them.
Big Bear

USA Leaders
May they first give away all their own money, property and
personal possessions.

Time
Time can heal, but, it don't pay the bills.

Security

Is one's inner relationship with the Great Spirit

Things

The best things in life are not things.

Possible Marriage Partner Warnings

You are attracted to partners that will repeat &
continue your families patterns of behavior,
especially the problem ones.

Avoid

Avoid getting sunburned.

Knowing Differences

Knowing in the mind is different than
Knowing in the heart.

Things Change

The more things change, the more they remain insane.

Yes / No?

Is anyone average? Is anyone typical?

Fans

Just because you like my stuff
doesn't mean I owe you anything.
Bob Dylan

Trouble

Trouble is cheap, to get into to, but expensive to get out of.

Truth
Truth stands, false falls.

Relationships
In any relationship in which two people become one,
the end result is two half people.
Wayne Dyer

Two-Faced
Look at a two faced person twice.

Vulture Respect
Vultures respect all life, waiting patiently,
with the gift of time, for death.

Wandering
Wandering the trail of life, wondering about life.

Real Philosopher
To be a real philosopher one must be able
to laugh at philosophy.
Blaire Pascal

Water
How can you miss the water till the well runs dry?

1863
Thirty-eight Santee Indians are hung,
largest mass hanging in US history.

Move

Get out of your own way.

Where to Stand

It is better to stand on the large boulder
than to be under it.

Worry

Most of what you worry about, never happens.

Poor / Ignorant

We can get over being poor,
but it takes longer to get over being ignorant.
Jane Sequichie Hifler

Timid

Are not women and children more timid than men?
Tonkahaska

Good People

Good people make the world better, and duller.

Bulges

Is that a gun in your pocket,
or are you just glad to see me.
Mae West

Baldness / Boldness

Baldness in love, Boldness in business.

Bargains

Make every bargain clear and plain
that none may afterwards complain.

Cats

Play with cats and get scratched.

Fame & Character

Fame is what you have taken, character's what you give,
when to this truth you waken, then you begin to live.
Bayard Taylor

Texas Law

Texas law - no walking in the streets if there is a sidewalk.

People Are Like The Moon

People are like the moon because
they have a light side and a dark side.

Business

Business is other people's money.

Attorneys & Vultures

The difference between attorneys and vultures is that
vultures wait till you're dead to pick you clean.

Admired

The rich are seldom admired by their servants.

Religious Drugs

Some people are with their religion as addicts
are with their drug.

Really!

Honest Lawyer Pub in Pahrump Nevada.

Brazil Money

February 1999 Brazil replaced it's central banker
for the second time in two weeks.

Bad

Nothing is all bad.

Paiute Speech On Justice in 1870

When white men rob stage, maybe kill somebody,
you send one sheriff to catch them, same way when
bad white men steal some cattle or horses.
When Injun does same thing, white man say
Injun on warpath, send soldiers to kill everybody.

Poverty

Poverty of course is no disgrace, but is damn annoying.
William Pitt

Blessed

Blessed is he who expects nothing
for he shall never be disappointed.
Alexander Pope

Healthy Relationship

Healthy relationship need and want separateness.

Boy

A boy is, of all wild beasts, the most difficult to manage.
Plato

Civilized Society

A civilized society is one which tolerates
eccentricity to the point of doubtful sanity.
Robert Frost

Better Check

When you see a light at the end of the tunnel,
better check to see if you're on a railroad track.

Bad Luck

My first wife divorced me and the second one won't.

Changing A Womans Mind

The best way to change a woman's mind
is to agree with her.

Recycle

Recycle everything.

Newspapers

There's seldom anything new in the newspapers.
Just the same things happening to different people.

Enlightenment

Enlightenment can be as easy as the rest of your life.

Lent

A good time to give up new year's resolutions.

Three Kinds Of People

There are three kinds of people: right-handed,
left-handed and underhanded.

Poor Advantage
The advantage to being poor is that it is inexpensive.

Double Enjoyment
He gave his girlfriend a sweater.

Talking Measurement
He who thinks by the inch and talks by the yard
deserves to be kicked by the foot.

Shakespeare
Shakespeare invented the words assassination and bump.

1853-56
The US whites takes 174 million acres of Indian lands
in 52 treaties, all are broken by US whites.

Blinking
Women blink almost twice as much as men do.

Don't
Don't use credit cards.

Sanity
One lie a day keeps sanity away.

Typewriter
Typewriter is the longest word that can be made using the
letters on only one row of the keyboard.

Words

Racecar and hayah read the same backwards.

Snails

A snail can sleep for 3 years.

English Speakers

China has more English speakers than the United States.

Smallest Country

Vatican City is the smallest country in the world, with a
population of 1000 and a size of 108.7 acres.

Material World

Lost and lodged in the material world.

Seeing

In a dark time, the eye begins to see.
Theodore Roethke

Birthdays

You share your birthday with at least 9 million
other people in the world.

Home

Home, to the small boy, is merely a filling station.

Peace

The white men & Indians kept fighting each other backward
and forward, and then I came in and made peace myself.
Santana

Overpopulation Need

The world is overpopulated with people
we need more Doctors.

Out Of Shape

When your muscles are soft and your arteries are hard.

New Miracle Drug Needed

A drug to cure you of all the side effects
from all the old miracle drugs.

Electric Chair

The electric chair was invented by a dentist.

Blush Changes

People usta blush when embarrassed
now they are embarrassed when they blush.

Tact

Some people have tact, others tell the truth.

Tunnel Vision

Tunnel vision is only great in a tunnel.

Good Cowboy Manners

Takin your boots off before puttin your feet on the table.

Praying, Preying

There's a difference between praying & preying
Some preachers do both.

Failure / Success
Failure isn't fatal and success isn't final.

Good Judgement
Good judgement comes from experience,
experience comes from bad judgement.

Doctors Tips
In case of amnesia, collect the fee in advance.

Courage
Courage is the ability to perceive what is.
Harry Palmer

Avoiding Alimony
Stay single or stay married.

Navy Luck
He joined the Navy to see the world
and got submarine duty.

Flyers
People who fly look down on people who don't.

Books
Never judge a book by its movie.

Los Angeles Clear Day
It's so beautiful on a clear day after the fog
lifts you can see the smog.

Avoid
Avoid hurting or harming anyone.

Movement
By too much sitting still the body becomes unhealthy,
and soon the mind.
Henry Wadsworth Longfellow

Tired
No one is as tired as the person who does nothing.

Originality
Originality is the art of concealing your source.

Solutions
"I must do something" will solve more problems
than "something must be done."

Happy
Make the choice to be happy!

Opportunity
I was seldom able to see an opportunity
until it ceased to be one.
Mark Twain

Progress
Progress is not the destruction of the rain forest.

Stock Exchange
When one buys, another sells, both think they are astute.

Law And Justice

This is a court of law, young man, not a court of justice.
Oliver Wendell Holmes Jr.

Father Swore

Calvin Coolidge was sworn in as president by his father.

Sex

Is sex dirty? Only if it's done right.
Woody Allen

Charlie Chan

One of the 13 actors who played Charlie Chan was of
Chinese ancestry.

Gary Grant

Gary Grant was an apostle of LSD.

Good Woman

Most good women are hidden treasures who
are safe because nobody looks for them.
Dorothy Parker

Oldest College

Harvard was founded in 1636.

Life

I don't want to earn my living; I want to live.
Oscar Wilde

Oscars

Tweety Pie won a Oscar in 1940.

Lawyers

A countryman between two lawyers is
like a fish between two cats.
Franklin

Gandhi

Mahatma Gandhi is buried in California

Great Spirit

We never quarrel about the Great Spirit
Cochise

Lost Faith

I have lost faith in America.
Martin Scheuler, whose daughter was killed at Kent State
1970

1864

New federal law allows Indians to
testify in trials against whites.

Life

If you wish to participate in life with any degree
of deliberation, your primary action must be to set a goal…
Commitment is backing up your primary with action.
Undertake something!
Harry Palmer

Popcorn

World's largest purchaser of popcorn is Cracker Jack.

Man

A mother takes twenty years to make a man of her boy,
and another woman makes a fool of him in twenty minutes.
Robert Frost

Outhouse Capital

Alaska has the most outhouses of any US state.

Neighbor

Do not hurt your neighbor,
for it is not him you wrong, but yourself.
The Shawnee

1868

US Commissioner of Indian Affairs estimates
that Indian wars in the west are costing the
government 1 million per Indian killed.

Poets

A poet can survive everything but a misprint.
Oscar Wilde

TV / Computers

Personal computers outsell TV's.

Dog Pill Instructions

Place the pill far back on the dogs tongue
and blow in its nose.

No Pun Intended

The average Rolling Stone is older than
the average GM executive.

Most Common Street in USA

Park Street is the most common.

Dollar Chews

Americans chew about a billion and a
half dollars worth of gum every year.

Prune Juice

Denver Colorado consumes the
least per person in the USA.

Source Of Life

They searched for a long time for the source of life, and
at last came to the thought that it issues from an invisible
creative power to which, they applied the name Wa-ko-da.
Playful Calf

Dynamite Peanuts

Peanuts are used in manufacturing dynamite.

Crime Arrests

The most popular crime arrest in America is drunk driving.

Farming

No race can prosper till it learns that there is
as much dignity in tilling a field as in writing a poem.
Booker T. Washington

Fate

That which God writes on thy forehead, thou wilt come to it.
Koran

In Love

In love, somehow, a man's heart is always either exceeding the speed limit, or getting parked in the wrong place.
Helen Rowland

Fear

Cruelty and fear shake hands together.
Balzac

Surprises In Nebraska

There are many surprises in Nebraska one of them is a town named Surprise.

USA Top 3 Religions

#1 Money #2 Sports #3 Politics.

Worry

Don't worry about anything you can't control and know you can't control anything.

Easier

It's easier to talk the talk than to walk the walk.

Wisdom

Wisdom is the ability to foresee the consequences of an action.
Harry Palmer

Fame

Nor fame I slight, nor for her favors call;
She comes unlooked for, if she comes at all.
Pope, Alexander

Sex And Aging
When younger, couldn't get enough, now, with aging, I can.

History
Your history lives in your body like a hidden organ,
influencing your life in every way.

Cowgirl's Laugh
A cowgirl's laugh is sweet as clover.

New York Pet Supplies
New York pet supplies included a bargain
designer dog bowl for only $750.

Best Life
The best life has to offer is life.

High Heels
High heels were invented by a woman
who had been kissed on the forehead.
Christopher Morley

Drink Only
Drink only from the bottle of love.

1868
Fourteenth Amendment to the constitution gives
Blacks the vote but specifically excludes Indians.

Joy
Joy - take it by the hand and walk with it.

Most Important Voice

The most important voice is that lone dissenting voice.

Stark Mad

Man is certainly stark mad: he cannot make a worm,
and yet he makes Gods by the dozen.
Michael Montaigne

1898 Kearney Cotton Mills
Nebraska Advertising Slogan

"Stand up for Nebraska by lying down
between Nebraska made sheets."

Speaking To A Group

When speaking to a group, there will be one who
argues with you. Your desire will be to silence him
but don't. He may be the only one listening.

Government Research

Farm pigs can become alcoholics.

Reality

They were those that would have wept to
step barefoot into reality.
Wallace Stevens

Fallin

We all fall, how far, ain't as important
as gettin up and standin tall.

Religion

There's nothing in Christianity or Buddhism that quite matches the sympathetic unselfishness of an oyster.
Hector Munro

Speak

Speak honestly or be silent.

Emergency Fund

Create an emergency fund so you can create an emergency.

Dad Takes Things Apart

Daughter: my dad takes things apart to see why they won't go. Date: So? Daughter: So you better go now.

Nothin Worse

Nothin worse than overdone tact.

Politicians

Politicians stay on their podium rather than stepping down among those they rob.

Give And Take

Take of the world as you find it, give of yourself as you are.

Key To Failure

The key to failure is trying to please everybody.
Bill Cosby

Mother

A mother is not a person to lean on, but a
person to make leaning unnecessary.
Dorothy Caufield Fisher

Indian Baptism

Holy Indian baptism of firewater.

Perfect

Nothing that is changing can be perfect.
Everything is changing.

Brains

Why don't women have men's brains?
Because they don't have penises to put them in.

Wean Yourself

Time to wean yourself from greed.

Love

Love doesn't knock and love doesn't have warning labels.

Southern Restaurant Coincidence

Only salt on tables of white, only pepper on tables of
blacks, salt & pepper only on mixed tables.

Power

Power is the ability to remain present and aware
and to shape reality.
Harry Palmer

Fools

For fools rush in where angels fear to tread.

20% Law Needed

20% reduction in all taxes each year.
20% reduction in all government each year.

Circle

The circle is complete.

Inner Child

When you get arrested tell them your inner child did it and
can't be prosecuted because he's a minor.

Good News

Scientists are near a breakthrough in technology
for retroactive abortions.

Cents

Cents of humor are rare.

Happiness Is Like A Kiss

Your gotta give it to someone else to get the
most good out of it yourself.

Enthusiasm

Lack of enthusiasm brings on sadness.

The Great Spirit

The Great Spirit placed us here
to take good care of Mother Earth,
all life, each other and ourselves.

Strength
Find the strength to enjoy your weaknesses.

Knowledge
Quietly hidden are those of greatest knowledge.

Hypocrites
Most people speak well of hypocrites.

History
Happy the people whose annals are blank in history books.
Carlyle

Politicians
Remember politician's allegiance is only to politics.

Hardship
The times are not so bad as they seem, they couldn't be.
Jay Franklin

Money Talks
Money talks a lot in Japanese.

Tax Complainers
People who complain about their taxes
are composed of two groups: men and women.

Customs
Customs are old habits.

Peace

May the peace of God which passes all understanding,
be with you now and always.

Eulogys

Eulogys teach us that people are better dead than alive.

Libraries

Nebraskans check out more books from libraries
and pay less than other states.

Progress

Progress takes a heavy toll.

Comparison

Compare 25,000 years use by Native Americans
to 500 years use by Europeans.

Statistics

Statistics are no substitute for judgement.
Henry Clay

Sound Of A Pig

There ain't no sound like a pig gettin cut.

Preparation H

Preparation H is being used to treat face wrinkles
quite successfully. Negative side effect: can
make you look like an ass.

Rights

We all got the right to be wrong.

Money

Money is better than poverty, if only for financial reasons.
Woody Allen

Smart Thief?

Steals toilet paper from large establishments and
resells on the street. No flashy cars, no flashy clothes,
no prestige. Makes a meager living and the risk
of being sent to prison for life is low.

Alcoholic Choices

1. Get sobered up. 2. Get locked up. 3. Get covered up.

Over

Nothings over till it's over.

Warpath

If I was goin on the warpath, it wouldn't be over there.
Sun Bear

Sweet Corn

Warning: eating sweet corn without ear worms
can cause hearing loss.

Christian Buddist

A really good Christian is a really
good Buddist and vice versa.

Crazy

Crazy as a rush hour commuter.

Cheap
He was so cheap that he wouldn't pay one dollar
to attend the last supper with the original cast.

Life
Life is kinda like squeezing laughter from an onion.

Political Promises
A promise is not a commitment.
NM Governor Bruce King

Fingerprints
Once upon a time there was two fingerprints
exactly the same, but only once.

Coos Bay Oregon Law
No possession of paint, ink, or chalk with
intent to apply graffiti.

Mistakes
Attorneys get paid for mistakes and doctors bury theirs.

Florida
July 1998 Florida - 67 counties in Florida all
but 1 currently affected by fires.

Paradise
American Indians 25,000 years in paradise
500 years of trouble in paradise.

Chicken Feet Exports

264,000 metric tons of US chicken feet exported to China last year.

Colored Milk

Yak milk is pink.

Safe Government

Whenever you can't feel safe with your government, you better leave them alone.
Fred Krzyzanowske, Sparks NE Rancher

Now

You are gonna die later so why not live now?

Wisdom

Wisdom is like stiff clay; you have to work it with your own hands before it becomes useful.
Harry Palmer

Success

A=Success then A=X+Y+Z. X is work, Y is play, Z is keep your mouth shut.
Albert Einstein

Daily

Finish everyday & be done with it.

Two Million Dollar Sleep Study

The results indicated that the average person needs 5 minutes more sleep.

Classic Lawyer Questions

Classic lawyer questions during a trial compiled
by "Massachusetts Bar Association Lawyers Journal".
1. Were you present when your picture was taken?
2. Were you alone or by yourself?
3. Was it you or your younger brother who
was killed in the war?
4. How far apart were the vehicles at the time of collision?
5. Did he kill you?
6. You were there until the time you left, is that true?

Women

You can't change a woman, but you can change women.

Unconditional Love

Doing the right thing for people irregardless
of who, what, when or where.

Problems

Root of many problems - the bottom line is money.

Simplify

Our life is frittered away by detail. Simplify, simplify.
Henry David Thoreau

Possessions & Activities

Too many possessions & activities get
in the way of enjoying life.

Two Kinds Of People

There are 2 kinds of people. Those who close
the outhouse door and those who don't.

Crazy
Crazy ain't insane.

Airsickness
The real cause of airsickness is the Wright Brothers.

Intimate Voice
His voice was as intimate as the rustle of sheets.
Dorothy Parker

Redneck Foreplay
Get in the truck bitch.

Desirable Movie
I want a movie that starts with an earthquake
and works up to a climax.
Samuel Goldwyn

Rest
No rest for the wicked and
the righteous don't need none.
David Lee (Pig Poet)

Pagan
Born again Pagan.

Recession / Depression
It's a recession when you neighbor loses his job;
it's a depression when you lose yours.
Harry Truman

More Stars

More than 100 billion stars in our galaxy,
and more than 100 billion galaxies.

Nebraska Brothel

Maggie Wheelock ran a brothel for
60 years in the Niobrara Valley.

Aging Wish

We just want to continue being a part of it all.

Limited Ambition

Their ambition was limited to getting something for nothin.

Genealogy

Genealogy is searching past generations to learn
who they were so we can understand who we are.

American Diet

Three quarters of American youth
will eat pizza for breakfast.

Judge Roy Bean

Judge Roy Bean ruled that a man killed by a
disreputable woman as suicide because, I had told
him if he fooled around with that woman he
was committing suicide and by God be did.

Marriage & Divorce

Marriage: legalized sex. Divorce: legalized pain.

Free Rides
There ain't no free rides.

Desire
I arise every morning torn between the desire to
save the world and the desire to savor the world.
It makes it hard to plan the day.
E. B. White

Luxuries
Most luxuries & comforts of life are not only
not indispensable, but positive hindrances
to the elevation of mankind.
Henry David Thoreau

Sick
Mostly we make ourselves sick.

Stonehenge
Give me that old time religion.

In The Sweetness Of Friendship
And in the sweetness of friendship let
there be laughter and the sharing of pleasure.
Kahlil Gibran

Real Work
The real work to be done on this planet is to make
ourselves more aware, to remind ourselves that our
essential nature is nonviolent, and to increase the amount
of compassion and cooperation on the planet.
Harry Palmer

Creation
God's creation, not, man's creation.

Religions
Someone else's spiritual vision, used & abused, substituted for seeking & receiving your own spiritual vision.

Plumbing
In plumbing a flush beats a full house.

Holocaust
American Indian Holocaust 10,000 times worse than Hitler.

Lawyers
"Virtue in the middle" said the Devil,
as he seated himself between two lawyers.

God
God. is, an abbreviation, for Goddess.

Poetry
Poetry is grace.

Impressing Women
Never try to impress a woman because if you do,
you'll have to keep up that standard the rest of your life.
W.C. Fields

Fun
The most important discipline.

Warpath

We do not take up the warpath without
a just cause and honest purpose.
Pushmataka

Hollywood Foreign Film

Native Americans "Dancing with wolves"

True God In America

The true God in America takes precedence over all
other false Gods, the true God is money.

I Love Animals

I love animals, they taste great.

Knocking

Neither love or death knock.

Most Important Things To Do

1. Doing nothing. 2. Messing around. 3. Dreaming.

Wisdom

Wisdom is knowing you're going
down the wrong path again.

Change

We must be the change that we wish to see in the world.

Coyote

Coyote (the trickster) is generally running the show.

Life, Death & Breath

Our first breath is an inhale, out last breath is an exhale.

Agreeable Friends

The most agreeable friends are animals. They ask no questions don't criticize and give unconditional love.

Lost

Lost in their minds.

How To Have A Blast At Work

Eat a very large serving of prunes before going to work.

Sign Makers

When sign makers go on strike,
is anything written on the signs?

Save A Cow

Save a cow, eat a vegetarian.

Town Rule

Great Grandfathers rule: Don't go to town - unless
- you've got something to sell.

Today

Today is my favorite day of the week.

Save Some Ozone

Want to save some ozone and reduce pollution?
Quit driving your car.

Slaves

Blacks, slaves to whites - Whites, slaves to greed.

Horse Feathers

Horse feathers gets a point across and is better in some circles but farmers and ranchers say something similar that lacks feathers cause horses don't have feathers and they don't eat birds.

Clinton

From almost a pervert to almost a convert.

USA Today

USA today 1/4 news (mostly bad) 1/4 money (mostly greed) 1/4 sports (mostly foolish) 1/4 Lifeline (mostly fun)

Spiritual Being

A spiritual being, having a human experience.

Older Than Me

Just a little older than me, he was young & wild & huntin trouble, so I jumped in and helped some.

Einstein

Einstein dreamed the theory of relativity.

1866

US Congress takes Indian lands to promote transcontinental railroad.

Dad's Last Words

My Dad's last words to my cousin Carla were - This dying is quite an experience, too bad I can't live to tell about it.

Iran Religious Chant

God is Great, Death to America.

Las Vegas

Las Vegas can easily make you a millionaire --
-- If -- you are a billionaire.

Prestigious Poverty

Celebrating prestigious poverty with flea market decor.

Jogging

Jogging - a healthy case of the runs.

Honorable

"Honorable" preceding the name of a judge,
Senator and such doesn't necessarily mean they are.

Sally Sez

Sally sez that sex is the only exercise
that's worth the bother.

Children

Children are not your second chance at life.

Doctor Translations

Let me check your medical history translates to I want to know if you've paid your, last bill before proceding.

Wisdom
Wisdom is gained from the pain of experience.

Under Every Smile
Under every smile is some sadness,
under every frown is some laughter.

Normal Week
A normal week on any farm and/or ranch is
that it isn't normal

1870
Grant transfers control of Indian agencies from army officers
to Christian missionaries.

Test Passed
The only test he ever passed with a high
score was the insanity test.

People
My Grandfather said "people are a lot like cattle,
if you open the gate and just stand there a bunch
of them will sort themselves."

Life Is Short
Life is short, even for tall people.

On Riches 1870
We do not want riches.
We want peace, and love.
Red Cloud

Fear
Fear is a belief in your inadequacy to deal with something.
Harry Palmer

French Crook
A French crook after release from jail asked the police to
return the $100,000 that he had stolen "honestly".

Happy
Happy as a pigged out pig.

Don't Believe
Don't believe everything you think.

Highway Ramp Repair
In 1998 a NY highway ramp connecting FDR Drive to
48th Street was reopened after being temporarily
closed for repair in 1987. 11 years and
11 million dollars worth of progress.

Astrological Sign
The astrological sign he was born under said "Emergency".

Marriage & Divorce
Presently it's still cheaper to get married than divorced
but the lawyers are promoting premarital agreements
to fix that situation.

Finer
Finer than frog fur.

Problem

When the problem is in your face, it's hard to
see the solution off in the sunrise.

Reason

There is a reason for them seasons.

Dope

I can't understand why anybody would want to devote
their life to a cause like dope. It's the most boring part of
me I can think of. It ranks a close second to television.
Frank Zappa

Last Word

The best way to get the last word is to apologize.

Government

The government taketh away 90%,
the government giveth away 10%.

Food Costs

Sixty percent of food cost is transportation.

James Dean

James Dean urinated in front of 2,000 people on a movie
set, explaining that if he could do that,
he could do anything in front of a camera.

Pushwater

Pushwater is the Indian word for gasoline.

False American Myth

George Washington was the first president of the U.S. Reality, John Hanson was the first under the articles of confederation. Hanson and seven other presidents have been forgotten.

Lance

Lance Sennette 1938-20__?
Favorite game: Hide the wienie.

Experience

Experience is one thing you can't get for nothing.

Paris, France

Dog doo doo and garbage in the streets.

Richest Man

1998 Bill Gates worth estimated at 60 billion. Forbes magazine reports a daily increase of about 40 million.

Estatic

Estatic only lasts a short time.

Marriage Expectations

Any expectation beyond companionship will be a problem.

History

History is mostly an ass struggle.

Give And Take

Some days we give more than we take.
Some days we take more than we give.

Poetree

Poetree grows from a poet's seed.

Real History

The book "American Holocaust" is real history
from journals & letters, such as Columbus'.

Right

It is dangerous to be right when the government is wrong.
Voltaire (1700's)

Lucille Ball

Lucille Ball was kicked out of drama
school for being too shy.

Women Want - Men Want

Women want "the fairy tale" - Men want "the tale"

Good Music

Most people wouldn't know good music
if it came up and bit them in the ass.
Frank Zappa

1871

Indians treaties were terminated by congressional action.

Dustin Hoffman

Dustin Hoffman was voted least likely to succeed by his classmates at the Playhouse Acting School.

Earth Angel

She was an angel with a broken wing.

Becoming

Don't let what you are being get in the way
of what you might become.
Harry Palmer

Offers

A man pretty much always refuses another man's
first offer, no matter what it is.
Mark Twain

Right Or Wrong

You could be as right as I am
or I could be as wrong as you are.

Dreams

Dreams are tomorrow, reality is today.

Fred Astarie

Fred Astarie's report read "can't act, slightly bald,
can dance a little" after his first screen test.

Poets

Life as a poet ain't easy, life with a poet ain't either.

Mom Said

My mom said at 83 that she hadn't ever
wanted to be poor again.

Helicopters

Hell i cop ters.

Forever Is

Forever is all the past. Forever is all the future.
Forever is not time or love. Forever is everything.
Forever is nothing but now.

Clinton's Motto

Don't get caught with your pants up.

Sign On Door

I have gone out to look for me, if I should get back
before I return, please hold me until I get here.

90% Breathing

90% of people breathe too shallow 90% of the time.

Now Is The Time

Now is the time to rearrange your mind.

1879

Carlisle Indian School begins removal of
Indian children from families to their boarding school.

Want

Don't want so much.

Viagra

Most insurance companies will pay for Viagra
but not for abortions.

President Jimmy Carter

First president to publicly admit to seeing a UFO.

Women

There are three kinds of women: the intelligent,
the beautiful and the majority.

Sanity Or Insanity?

Settling in and succeeding in this societies insanities
held sacred that are insane.

Round

Everything tries to be round.
Black Elk

Nothin Whiter

Ain't nothin whiter than a white
white girl loved by a dark black boy.

Memories

Old memories keep us young.

Hidden

Treasure is hidden under ground,
Joy is hidden under sorrow.

Seek

Seek & ye shall find.

Insane Asylum

Do you think earth was designed to be
the insane asylum for the universe?

Breaking Up

Women initiate the break-up 70% of the time.

World's Largest Grain Elevator

The world's largest grain elevator is in Hutchinson Kansas.

My Father Said

"When I was young, some days were better than others.
Now I'm old and some days are worse than others."

Optimists

Optimists view evil as positive and necessary.

Looking For A Husband

When a woman is looking for a husband
he is either single or married.

The System

The system is collapsing from the heavy weight of greed.

World's First TV Dinner

The world's first TV dinner was created
by a Nebraskan named Gerry Thomas.

Forgiveness

Years from forgiveness.

Change
Life is always in a phase of change,
and U gotta change too.

Teenage Boys
Teenage boys wanting to be men, too serious to be funny.

Majority
Whenever you find yourself on the side of the
majority, it is time to pause & reflect.
Mark Twain

Tears
Tears are needed for rainbows.

Possessions
That which you cannot give away,
you do not possess. It possesses you.
Iven Ball

Do
Lighten up!

Peace
When you make peace with who you are,
you'll be content with what you have.
Doris Mortman

Room
There is always room in the top one percent.

Fear / Faith
Fear clogs; Faith liberates.
Elbert Hubbard

Size
One size fits none.

Enemy
You have met the enemy, you are the enemy.

Success
The secret to her success was she made
you happy that you'd been taken.

New Idea
When someone floats a new idea do you try to puncture it?

Desire To Discover
Our desire to discover is to rediscover those simple
early places our hearts first opened to.

Kamikaze
The divine wind.

Saint Teresa
From silly devotions and from sour -
faced saints, good God, deliver us.
Saint Teresa

Language
The language of the heart is the language of all life.

Worldwide Awakening

When enough people are able to see that the only real differences between any of us are the ideas and beliefs that we create, there will be a spontaneous worldwide awakening to the fact that we share an inseparable destiny.
Harry Palmer

Young

When young, we were, really cool,
real busy, being, the fool.

Golden Arch

She was a golden arch from here to eternity.

Emotional Excitement

Emotional excitement is often confused
with spiritual experience.

Word

A word, once spoken, can not be retrieved.

Winners

We can all be winners.

Arizona Desert Kangaroo Rat

The Arizona Desert Kangaroo Rat hibernates for months
and/or years, emerging only when it rains.

Luck

He who does not venture has no luck.

Life
Mother Earth receives the love of Father Sun.
All life is dependent on that love.

Talks
He who talks much errs much.

Experience
That which you receive in the greatest quantity,
shortly after, you really needed it.

Flee
To flee and to run are not the same.

Opportunities
Opportunities are usually disguised as hard work,
so most people don't recognize them.
Ann Landers

Servants
He who has servants has unavoidable enemies.

Sooner Or Later
Sooner or later I'm going to die, but I'm not going to retire.
Margaret Mead

Saints
This world praises dead saints and persecutes living ones.

Trust
It's easy to trust the cat after you put the cream out of reach.

Retirement

Retirement at sixty-five is ridiculous.
When I was sixty-five I still had pimples.
George Burns

New / Old

The new pleases and the old satisfies.

Faults

Rare is the person who can weigh the faults
of another without putting his thumb on the scales.

Speaking / Listening

He who speaks sows, and he who listens harvests.

Virtues

Virtues all agree, but vices fight one another.

Fate

If fate throws a knife at you, there are two ways
of catching it: by the blade or by the handle.

Lie Flies

A lie flies til it is overtaken by truth.

Flattery

He who flatters you wants to cheat you or wants your help.

Dumb / Smart

Too dumb to be a cowboy
Too smart to be a farmer.

Listening

If I listen I have the advantage, if I speak others have it.

For Sale

Lousy Cow Hay, sold to me as good horse hay by "trusted neighbor" for information call Lena Fox 545-8350.

Grief

Grief shared is half grief, joy shared is double joy.

History

The most important history to study is that which was forgotten or swept under the carpet.

Laugh At Government

It will still cost the same money but the mental strain is lighter if you laugh.

IBP

The worlds largest slaughter house company for beef & pork.

Bloody Mary

A Bloody Mary without alcohol in Kentucky is called a Bloody Shame.

Gratitude

Gratitude opens a crack in consciousness that lets grace in. Being grateful opens you to grace. Complaining, judging, resisting, all lead to suffering.
Harry Palmer

Omaha, NE

Omaha Nebraska had the first indoor shopping mall.

Corn To Meat

One 56 pound bushel of corn makes 5.6 pounds of beef, 13 pounds of pork, 28 pound of catfish, 32 pounds of chicken.

Luxuries

Luxuries of yesterday are necessities of today.

Milker

A cow milker by hand can milk six an hour,
by machine a hundred.

Work

Work towards creative solutions that will benefit all.

Trust

Only the faithless can be trusted.

Old Lakota

The old Lakota was wise. He knew that man's
heart away from nature becomes hard.
Standing Bear

Learning

Society today is a reflection of the fact
that we haven't learned from history.

Eating

Big dogs eating little dogs in the quest of the sacred dollar.

Big Rain

When it rained for 40 day and 40 nites, it totaled over
400 inches where Noah was, in Arizona
it rained almost a quarter of a inch.

Rise

Rise to your highest level of incompetence.

1879

First US court decision that an Indian is a person
within the meaning of law in the United States.
Standing Bear, Ponca Indian, Omaha NE

Aging

You regret all those mistakes resisting temptation.

Last Words

James Rodques, before the firing squad, when asked if he
had a final request. "Why yes, a bullet-proof vest."

Nothing Is Illegal

Nothing is illegal if sanctioned by government.

Sacred Cows

Sacred cows make great hamburgers.
Robert Risner

Money

So you think money is the root of all evil.
Have you ever asked what is the root of money?
Ayn Rand

Names

Mrs. Screech teaches singing in British Columbia.

The Establishment

You may give us your symptoms, we will make the diagnosis. And we, the establishment - for which I make no apologies for being a part of - will implement the crime.
Spiro T Agnew

God

Everyone you meet is a God in disguise.

Silence

Silence is holy.

Henry Ford II

Don't complain. Don't explain.
Henry Ford II

Working For A Large Company

Going to work for a large company is like getting on a train. Are you going sixty miles an hour or is the train going sixty miles an hour and you're sitting still?
S. Paul Getty

Hypocrisy

An ounce of hypocrisy is worth a pound of ambition.
Michael Karda

Living

The cost of living is going up and the chance of living is going down.
Flip Wilson

No Cure

There is no cure for death.

Non-Conformist

Non-conformists hate non-conformists who are not conforming to their standards of non-conformity.

Holy Grail

Gross national product is our Holy Grail.
Stewart Udall

Bird Forecast

Birds are noisier before a storm.

Fortune

Fortune favors the brave.

Great Men

Few great man could pass personnel.
Paul Goodman

Organic Cowboy

Works in BS all week
Talks BS Saturday night
Hears BS Sunday morning

Pablo Picasso

I'd like to live like a poor man with lots of money.
Pablo Picasso

Civilization

Civilization is unbearable, but it is "less"
unbearable at the top.
Timothy Leary

Money

Money is like manure,
you have to spread it around or it smells.
J. Paul Getty

Buddhistic Calm

There is a certain Buddhistic calm that comes
from having - money in the bank.
Tom Robbins

1885

The last great herd of buffalo is killed

To Succeed

To succeed it is necessary to accept the world
as it is and rise above it.
Michael Korda

The Road

Sometimes the mud is deep,
trudging the road of happy destiny.

Rat Race

The trouble with the rat race is that
even if you win, you're still a rat.
Lily Tomlin

Be Nice

Be awful nice to 'em going up, because
you're gonna meet 'em all comin' down.
Jimmy Durante

Your Intellect & Reality

When you can experience yourself as distinct from
the intellect, you are able to see the patterns of
assumptions and beliefs that filter and distort your
understanding of (and control over) reality.
Harry Palmer

Everyone Is Willing

Willing to do it or willing to watch someone else do it.

Transformation

It is easier to make a businessman out of a musician
than a musician out of a businessman.
Goddard Lieberman

Anger Threat

I'm so mad, I won't tell you how I feel.

Humans

Humans differ but their foundations of
human nature are the same.

Leadership

Leadership appears to be the art of getting others to want
to do something you are convinced should be done.
Vance Packard

Indulgences

Indulgences are straying from your spiritual path.

First Woman

I was the first woman to burn my bra,
it took the fire department four days to put it out.
Dolly Parton

Future

The future is a convenient place for dreams.
Anotole France

Liberated Woman

Once upon a time, a liberated woman was someone
who had sex before marriage and a job afterward.
Gloria Steinem

Incompetence

Man cannot live by incompetence alone.
Laurence, Peter

Two Kinds Of Women

There are two kinds of women: those who want
power in the world, and those who want power in bed.
Jacqueline Kennedy Onassis

Anatomy

Anatomy is destiny.
Sigmund Freud

Problem / Solution

Everyone is part of the problem, few are part of the solution.

Sensitive Cowboy

He asked his girlfriend upon her return from
the restroom if everything had come out OK.

God Made Man

God made man, and then said I can do
better than that and made woman.
Adela Rogers St. John

Daughter

A daughter is an embarrassing and ticklish possession.
Menander

Facts

Don't let the facts keep you from doin what you gotta do.

Songs

Our songs are part of nature, life.
American Indian

Free

Free to be you and me.
Marlo Thomas

Love

I'm nobody's steady date. I can always be distracted
by love, but eventually I get horny for my creativity.
Gilda Radner

Right

We have a right to our own bodies.
Shere Hite

Woman Myth

The myth of the strong black woman is the other side
of the coin of the myth of the beautiful dumb blonde.
Eldridge Clever

1886

Geronimo surrenders, ending the Indian wars

Consenting

One can never consent to creep when
one feels an impulse to soar.
Helen Keller

Men

There are men I could spend eternity with, but not this life.
Kathleen Norris

Barbara Ann

Barbara Ann once said
"Over 95% of what we do is unnecessary."

Attitude

Attitude is everything.

Sex

Sex is one of the nine reasons for reincarnation,
the other eight are unimportant.
Henry Miller

Men

Men are like bob-wire, they got their good points.

Fame

Popularity? It is glory's small change.
Victor Hugo

Chastity

The most unnatural of the sexual perversions.
Aldous Huxley

Mother Earth

The pulse of Mother Earth
slows our own in a calming way.

Dangerous

I'm dangerous, I think.

Right Or Wrong

If it don't feel right, it ain't right.

Tell Them

Tell them how we loved all that was beautiful.
American Indian

Growing Old

The River flows around the bend
and in a moment we grow old.

Men

It's not the men in my life that counts, it's the life in my men.
Mae West

Justifiable Suicide

Suicide is justifiable only in self defense.

American Fitness

15 million a year on diet sodas,
8 million a year on fitness clubs.

Faults

I may have faults but being wrong ain't one of them.
Jimmy Hoffa

Freedoms

Freedom's just another word for nothing left to lose.
Kris Kristofferson

Relativity

When a man sits with a pretty girl for an hour,
it seems like a minute. But let him sit on a hot stone
for a minute, and it's longer than any hour.
That's relativity.
Albert Einstein

Men

The difference between men
and boys is the price of their toys.

Quarrel

We may quarrel with men about things on earth,
but we never quarrel about the Great Spirit.
Chief Joseph

Details

We think in generalities, but we live in detail.
Alfred North Whitehead

Man's Heart

The royal road to a man's heart is to talk to
him about the things he treasures most.
Dale Carnegie

Giving

He wouldn't give you standin room in hell.

Cancer Cells

An example of growth for growth's sake,
and they even look like a city.

Flounderin

A lifetime flounderin in the mire of sin.

Empty

Empty as church on Saturday nite.

1887
Congress passes the Great Allotment Act
(The Dames Act). Tribes lose millions of acres

Humans
Humans aren't the only species on Earth,
they just act like it.

Herd Singer
Just singin to run off the coyotes.

Spaceship
We are all on a spaceship and that spaceship is Earth.
Four billion passengers, and no skippers.
Wernher Von Braun

Lower
Lower than a toad in a post hole.

Women
Women are meant to be lovely, not to be understood.
Oscar Wilde

Rich
Had enough money to burn a wet mule.

Living
Live as if you expected to live a hundred years,
but might die tomorrow.
Ann Lee

Sanctuaries

This Mother Earth, all life, all creation and
ourselves are natural sanctuaries.

Law

Laws grind the poor, and rich men rule the law.
Goldsmith

Men Masturbating

Why do men masturbate? It's sex with someone they love.

Somewhere

Somewhere, something incredible is waiting to be known.
Carl Sagan

Struttin

Struttin like a turkey gobbler with a flock of hens.

Revolutionary

The first duty of a revolutionary is to get away with it.
Abbie Hoffman

Reserved Seat

By the time he was thirty he had a reserved seat in hell.

His Wife

His wife was more ornamental than useful.

Driest Summer

At the end the of driest summer we
had a herd of jerky on the hoof.

Indian Prayer

Jesus, please protect me from your followers.

Growing Old

In growing old, one grows more foolish and wise.

Sin

An ancient archery term, meaning, off the mark. Applied
to your spiritual path, sin means, your heart's not in it.

Quiet

Quiet as a horse thief after a hangin.

Raised

He was raised on prunes & proverbs.

Youth

He was young & wanted to wear out a couple
more saddles before picking out a corral.

His Religion

Most of his religion was in his wifes name.

Eyesight

He couldn't see whose calves he was ketchin
but he could see where to brand 'em.

Scarce

Scarce as bird poop in a cuckoo clock.

1889

Two million acres of Indian territory (Oklahoma)
are givin to whites.

Slower

Slower than a snail on crutches.

Cow Smart

As cattle smart as a calf's mother.

Medical Services

The homeless, the poor and the uninsured,
do without medical services while prison inmates
are given free medical & dental services.

Cunning

As cunning as a she-wolf with pups.

Striking Women

I have never struck a woman.
Never! Not even my poor old mother.
W.C. Fields

Cowboy Transformation

The old cowboy tore a leaf out of the prayer book
& commenced buildin a new life of Bull Durham.

Mind

Pass safely across the uncharted turbulence
of the mind into the region of the soul.
Harry Palmer

Soft

Soft as bear grease.

Happy

Happy as a hog bein drug away from a feed trough.

Doctors & Illness

If it ain't life threatening, wait a week
most illness will heal themselves.

Welcome

Welcome as a tax collector.

Slicker

Slicker than a bare clay hill after a rain.

Straight

Straight as a wagon tongue.

Red

Progressed from worrying about reds being in this county
to worrying about this country being in the red.

Optimist

Optimist dealing with reality.
Pessimist?

Comfortable
Comfortable as a horse thief at a hangin tree.

War
The USA has destroyed several countries in war,
then rebuilt them to take away
America business and workers.

Lawyers
A lawyers greatest asset is his lie, ability.

Dress
Be careless in your dress if you must, but keep a tidy soul.
Mark Twain

Buying
Don't buy anything you don't need.

Justice
Any man in ancient Greece who was committed of
kissing a women in public was given the death sentence.

Socks
Wrap the lower part of a sock around your fist
and a correct sized socks heel will just meet the toe.

Death
I'm not afraid to die. I just don't want to
be there when it happens.
Woody Allen

Poker

The best time to bluff is right after
winning more than one pot.

Love

Ordinary human love is capable of raising man
to the experience of real love.
Hakin Jami, Sufi

Limited Rights

Our rights are limited to where another's begin.

Mules

Mules are smarter and
more sure footed than horses.

Scattered

Scattered like a bunch of snowbirds.

Illness Causes

20% not breathing enough air.
20% not drinking enough water.
20% not getting enough exercise.
20% not getting enough nutrients.
20% other causes.

Recognition

I'd recognize him in hell with his hide burned off.

Cockroaches

A dozen cockroaches can live on the
glue of a stamp for one week.

1890

US Indian population reaches low of 250,000.

Storm Distance

A thunderstorms distance in miles equals the
number of seconds between the lightening
and the thunder divided by five.

Eyesight

Houseflies can only see you three feet away.

Nerds

Real nerds don't know they are nerds.

Seattle

Non-summer rainy days in Seattle
equal sunny days in summer.

Art

You are your own work of art.

Smelled

Smelled worse than a wolf den.

Demonstrators

Those who stay at a demonstration when it starts
to rain are the ones you can count on.

Lard

An adult Black Bear makes 12 gallon of lard.

College

Succeed at college by doing all the
homework on the day it is assigned.

Horses

The most important thing on a horse is good feet.

Music Bridge

Music bridges the differences in culture and people.

Largest Enchilada

Every year, Las Crucens work together to make the world's
largest enchilada at the Whole Enchilada Fiesta.

Advertising

Business adverting should exceed
10% of sales for the first 20 years.

Onions

Planting onions - the smaller the set, the larger the onion.

Spit

Forty below or colder and spit freezes
before hitting the ground.

Lost

When lost, travel downstream.

Youth

The youngest has the longest eyelashes.

Weddings

The more extravagant the wedding the
shorter the marriage.

Anger

It's hard to shake hands with an angry fist.

Survival

Three minutes without air, three days without water,
three weeks without food.

Market Forecasting

The market goes up and down with womens skirts.

Sailing

Red sun at nite, sailors delight;
Red sun in the morning, sailor take warning.

Dating

The way your new date treats service
people is the way you'll be treated later.

Most Models

Anything that fits most models won't fit yours.

Voting

Appearance & manner win 2/3 of the vote while
competence & experience win 1/3 of the vote.
A hero can nullify the above and win.

Writing

Two handwritten pages make one typewritten.

Indecision

If you can't decide what you want and need,
you need sleep.

Pigs Rule

Sheep ruled by pigs.

Marriage

A young man marries for sex. A middle aged man marries
for companionship. An elderly man marries for a nurse.

Auto Rattle

The most common auto rattle is the exhaust system.

Suggested Changes

Change your resentments into acceptance
Change your anger into love
Change your fear into hope

Surgeons Opportunity

Personality transplants.

Venture Capitalist

Venture capitalists want a return of 5-10
times their investment in 3-5 years.

Cut & Run

Cut & run business - cut losses now, let profits run.

Trout

Native trout have whole fins,
hatchery trout have ragged fins.

No Farms, No Grocery Stores

The Australian Aborigines eat "whatever presents itself to them" in an attitude of trust and reception.

Dangerous

Those claiming God is on their side are dangerous as hell.

Teacher Quality

Any teacher who sez their students are all dumb is a poor teacher.

Extinct

Extinct is probably forever.

Pearls

A real pearl will grate when rubbed against your teeth, a fake will feel smooth.

1891

Congress authorizes leasing by whites of Indian lands.

Spiderweb Forecasting

Drops of drew in evening spiderwebs mean good haying weather tomorrow.

People

Different stokes for different folks.

Habits

Nothing so needs reforming as other peoples habits.
Mark Twain

Showers
A five minute shower is worth an hour's sleep.

Higher Power
You need to have a higher power
and to make sure you're not it.

Fall
Fall colors in the east move south about 50 miles a day.

Mother Earth
Honor Mother Earth.

Stocks
Stocks that fall the most in a down cycle
will rise the most in the next up cycle.

Horse Forecast
When a horse yawns, the weather will change.

Tire Pressure
Your car tires will drop one pound in air pressure
for each ten degree drop in air temperature.

Fads
A Canadian fad takes a year to catch on in America.

Travel Plans
When traveling double the money
and half the activities you planned.

Spring
Spring moves north about 13 miles a day.

Experience
No man was ever so completely skilled in the
conduct of life, as not to receive new information
from age and experience.
Terence

The Price Of Learning
Experience teaches us at the expense of our illusions.

Fast Food
Fast food restaurants sell about
half their sales at the drive thru.

Manners
People short on manners are short on most everything.

Life
Life is a song/dance for a heart that is free.

Draft
The draft is white people sending black people
to fight yellow people to protect the
country they stole from red people.
Hair

Hollywood Employment
Drug addicts are promoted, conservatives are fired.

Murder

You mean you can get away with murder in this country?
Bernard Miller, whose son was killed at Kent State 1970

Talkin

Too much talkin can get in the way of most everything.

Love

In love, one always begins by deceiving oneself,
and one always ends by deceiving others;
that Is what the world calls a romance.
Oscar Wilde

Sharing

Share your experience and hope, not your prejudices.

I.O.U.

Nobody's I.O.U. is as good as their cash.

Hate

I have never hated a man enough to
give his diamonds back.
Zsa Zsa Gabor

Addicts Humor

You know what's so funny about addicts?
We think we're not!
Anne Wilson Schaef

Love

Love is so much better when you are not married.
Maria Callas

Oriental Carpet

Be careful when you walk on an Oriental carpet because you're stepping on someone's psychedelic vision.
Timothy Leary

Solitude

Solitude is un-American.
Erica Jong

Women

I always run into strong women who are looking for weak men to dominate them.
Andy Warhol

Security

Security is mostly superstition.
Helen Keller

Beatle Knowledge

People think the Beatles know what's going on.
We don't. We're just doing it.
John Lennon

Swinging

If you swing both ways, you really swing.
I just figure, you know, double your pleasure.
Joan Baez

Inside

Inside every fat Englishman is a thin Hindu trying to get out.
Timothy Leary

Desire

Never let go of the fiery sadness called desire.
Patti Smith

Freedom

No one's free, even the birds are chained to the sky.
Bob Dylan

Perfection

You are perfect exactly the way you are.
Werner Erhard

Insanity

A perfectly rational adjustment to an insane world.
R.D. Lang

Obstacles

Looking back, my life seems like one long obstacle race,
with me as its chief obstacle.
Jack Parr

1906

Federal government seizes 50,000 acres of Indian land
including Sacred Blue Lake of Taos Pueblo, NM.

Security

Only the insecure strive for security.
Wayne Dyer

Importance

I am more important than my problems.
Jose Ferrer

Facts

Facts do not cease to exist because they are ignored.
Aldous Huxley

Laughing Or Crying

Laughing or crying is what a human being
does when there's nothing else he can do.
Kurt Vonnegut, Jr.

Dependency

I can't live without that blanket. I can't face life unarmed.
Linus

Trouble

Trouble is the common denominator of living.
It is the great equalizer.
Ann Landers

Source

We all come from the same source and return to the same
source.

Fighting With Fire

People who fight fire with fire usually end up with ashes.
Abigail Van Buren

Advice

Keep your advice quiet till it's requested then keep it short.

Manhattan, KS Law

No indoor furniture on outdoor porches.

Loss

Death is not the greatest loss in life. The greatest
loss is what dies inside us while we live.
Norman Cousins

Wonderful

Wonderful people do not always make wonderful parents.
Abraham Maslow

Southwest History

New Mexico State University's first scheduled graduation
was canceled when the sole member of the
senior class was killed in a gunfight.

Children

Do not mistake a child for his symptom.
Erik Erikson

Humor

Funny had better be sad somewhere.
Jerry Lewis

TV

Chewing gum for the eyes.
Frank Lloyd Wright

Reality

Reality is a movie.
Abbie Hoffman

Deodorant
There's no deodorant like success.
Liz Taylor

Politics
The end move in politics is always to pick up a gun.
R. Buckminster Fuller

Folly
The follies which a man regrets the most in life are those
which be didn't commit when he had the opportunity.
Helen Rowland

Television
Television has proved that people will
look at anything rather than each other.
Ann Landers

Love
Either take away, O Eros, all wish for love,
or let me be loved: Take away all desire, or satisfy it.
Lucilius

Man
The real difference between men is not sanity and insanity,
but more or less insanity.

Farming
It makes but little difference whether you
are committed to a farm or a county jail.
Henry David Thoreau

Truth

The truth is the one thing nobody will believe.
George Bernard Shaw

Tainted Money

His money is twice tainted: taint yours and taint mine.
Mark Twain

Failure

Our greatest glory is not in never falling
but in rising every time we fall.
Confucius

Fully Living

When we realize how precious life is, our desire to live fully
in the present will be strong enough to let go of the past
and not obsess about the future.
Harry Palmer

Position

Always stay in your own movie.
Ken Kesey

Male / Female

An actor, is something less than a man, while
an actress is something more than a woman.
Richard Burton

Time

Whatever begins, also ends.
Seneca

Money / Acting

If someone is dumb enough to offer me
a million dollars to make a picture,
I am certainly not dumb enough to turn it down.
Liz Taylor

Politics

Politics is sex in a hula hoop.
Richard Reeves

Talking

Don't say anything unless you can improve on silence.

Streets Of Philly

The streets are safe in Philadelphia, it's
only the people who make them unsafe.
Frank Rizzo, Mayor

Money

Money is the mother's milk of politics.
Jessee Unruh

Thinkin

To much thinkin can ruin the whole deal.

Diplomacy

The art of jumping into trouble without making a splash.
Art Linkletter

Human Rights

There are no human rights in Uganda.
Idi Arnin

Government

Put a bullet in a guy's head,
and he won't bother you any more.
Attorney General William Janklow

Never Ask

Never ask a man the size of his ------- anything.

Game

The game women play is men.
Adam Smith

Prisoners Of War

Prisoners of war for 500 years, the American Indians.

Those Who Know

Those who know most everything are too
young to know much of anything.

Fight

You don't have to go to every fight you're invited to.

Grease It

Grease it before it squeaks.

When

When the sun's shinin, Hay.
When the music's playin, Dance.

One Of These Days

One of these days never comes.

1909

Theodore Roosevelt issues eight executive orders transferring 2.5 million acres of Indian lands to national forests, two days before leaving presidency.

Revenge

Get away, forget it, life will get even with 'em.

Facts

Statin the facts ain't braggin.

Schooling

I have never let my schooling interfere with my education.
Mark Twain

Military Intelligence

Military intelligence is a contradiction in terms.
Groucho Marx

Truth Shared

Truth shared leads others to truth.

Sorrows Grow

Sorrows grow bigger and multiply in alcohol & drugs.

Fix Yourself

Fix yourself rather than others.

Three Classes Of People

There are three classes of people: the haves,
the have-nots, and the charge-its.

Fool

A fool and his money are soon married.

Trouble

Sometimes you can't keep trouble from comin round
but you don't have to go out chasin it.

Helpin

The closest you can come to helpin most
folks is to stay outta their way.

1910

Federal government forbids the Sun Dance among Indians.

Good Reason

If there ain't a good reason to do something,
then that's a pretty good reason not to do it.

No

If you're gonna say no, the sooner the better.

Two Kinds Of People

There's two kinds of people, those who believe
that and those who know better.

New And Improved

New and improved usually ain't.

Puppy Love

Puppy love can lead to a dog's life.

Temptation
Temptation comes round more than opportunity.

Life
Accepting life on life's terms is kinda hard, like growin up.

Love
Leavin behind somethin you love
is sometimes hard but necessary.

Nobody Knows
Nobody knows it all, including you.

Nature
Nature is the only teacher.

Men Are Stronger
Men are stronger, women are weaker and visa versa.

Cowboys
Everything bad you've heard about cowboys
is true but they mostly take care of the cows.

Hard Boiled
Most hard boiled people are half baked.

Disagreeable
Don't be disagreeable just because you disagree.

Virtue
Virtue is it's own punishment.

Humor

Humor dilutes pain.

Smart / Dumb

You see an awful lot of smart guys with dumb women,
but you hardly ever see a smart woman with a dumb guy.
Erica Jong

Gossip

Those who gossip to you, will gossip of you.

Laughter

Laughter is like premium gasoline,
it helps take the knock out of living.

Fool

Sometimes the fool is right.

Black Elk 1912

Again - I recall the great vision you sent me.
It may be that some little root of the sacred tree still lives.
Black Elk

Speed Zone

"Speed zone ahead" does not mean pedal to the metal.

Do Not Pass

"Do not pass" does not mean stop
and wait for the sign to be removed.

You're Gonna Get

You're gonna get about what you expect
depending on your attitude and work.

Love

The only thing more tragic than to love is not to love.

Jobs

There are really not many jobs that actually
require a penis or a vagina, and all other
occupations should be open to everyone.
Gloria Steinem

Losers

Losers lose because they don't do what winners do.

Progress

Most real progress comes from
one person working alone.

Adversity

In the adversity of our best friends we often find
something that is not exactly displeasing.
La Rochefoucauld

Seeing God

God is everywhere, in everything, in you.
Look in the mirror and see God.

Ideas

Good ideas require immediate action.

Sex

Would you encourage your mate to have sex with someone if you were guaranteed to get a million dollars?

Compliment

Compliment more than three people every day.

Watch

Watch the sunrise. Watch the sunset. Watch the moonrise. Watch the moonset. Watch the clouds. Watch the stars.

Celebrate

Celebrate other people's birthdays.

Do

Look people in the eyes. Say thank you often. Say please often. Be the first to say hello.

Leave Everything

Try to leave everything better than you found it.

Gasoline

Run your vehicle on the top half of the tank.

Sugar Killer

Americans eat an average of 125 pounds of sugar a year.

Power

Never underestimate the power of love, forgiveness and prayer.

Polite

Be polite to everyone.

Harry Truman's First Job

Harry's first job was playing the piano in Kansas City
in a Pendegas generated palace of gambling,
drinking and prostitution.

Honesty

Don't believe those who say how honest they are.

Listen

Listen to street poets and musicians, leave a donation.

Needs

I always had a repulsive sort of need
to be something more than human.
David Bowie

Punctuality

Start everything on time.

Seeking

You can get anything you want at Alice's Restaurant.
Arlo Guthrie

Youth

There isn't anything wrong with youth that time can't cure.

Better

Make everything better not bigger.

Sobriety

The fun thing about being sober is meeting all the friends
I've had for years - especially the ones I've never met.
Alice Cooper

Revenge

Revenge is often like hitting a dog because the dog bit you.
Austin O'Malley

Limits

Reality has limits; stupidity has not.
Napoleon

Rope

Spinning a rope is a lot of fun, providing your neck ain't in it.
Will Rogers

Scenic Route

Take the scenic route.

1913

Federal government issues Indian
Head nickel with Buffalo on other side.

Regret

Regret is a break in higher-self trust.
You stop trusting that your higher self is creating
the experience that it needs for its own evolvement.
Harry Palmer

Burma Shave

**1st sign: DINAH DOESN'T 2nd sign: TREAT HIM RIGHT
3rd sign: BUT IF HE'D SHAVE 4th sign: DINAH-MITE!
5th Sign: BURMA SHAVE**

Doing

Do what needs to be done when it needs to be done.

Self Pity

Don't wallow in self pity, take action, do something
nice for someone else.

Religion

Be knowledgeable and tolerant of other people's religions.

Knowledge

Everyone knows things you don't know.

Humor

Humor heals.

Life

In life it's better to move & bend than to break
from the wind of hard knocks.

Richest

The richest is the one with the cheapest pleasures.

Peace

You can't herd the people of the world onto
the path of peace with dogs of war.

Habits
Your habits are your friends and your enemies.

Worry
Worry is compulsive recycling of negative thoughts.

Contentment
Be content with what you have.

Serenity Prayer
God grant me the serenity to accept the things
I cannot change; the courage to change the things I can;
and the wisdom to know the difference.
Reinhold Niebuhr

Meditation
Meditation or Medication!

Possessions
To be content with little is hard, to be
content with much is harder.

Power
Will power won't power supreme power.

Troubles
Don't advertise your troubles, there's no market.

Ships
It isn't the ship in the water but the
water in the ship that sinks it.

Misery

It isn't miserable to be blind; it is miserable
to be incapable of enduring blindness.
Helen Keller

Women

Women are here to stay, make the best of them.

Discontentment

Discontentment with others is mostly caused
by discontentment with ourselves.

Mistakes

A mistake is proof that someone tried to do something.

Doing

You can't do everything at once,
but you can do something at once.

Life

Life is 10% what you make it and 90% how you take it.

1917

US Governments lifts restrictions allotments,
launching "Forced patent" period.
Thousands of Indians lose their land.

Love

As you love yourself and others, you will be loved.

Housework

Housework is work unnoticed until it isn't done.

Talking

Always close your mouth before someone else wants to.

Doing

One thing at a time and that done well
is a very good rule as many can tell.

Mistakes

Learn from the mistakes of others,
you can't live long enough to make them all yourself.

Luck

Your luck is how you treat others.

Needs

So many Gods, so many creeds, so many paths
that wind and wind when just the art of
being kind is all the sad world needs.

Goal

Make your goal, simplicity, serenity and sincerity.

Faithful Husband

A faithful husband is one whose
alimony check is always on time.

Six Foot Birth

Newborn giraffes fall six feet and hit the ground at birth.

Be

Be what you wish others to become.

Life

Life is not the candle, it is the burning.

Knowledge

Know enough to know enough not to.

Judgement

Be to others virtues very kind,
be to others faults a little blind.

End Of Your Rope

When you get to the end of your rope,
tie a knot in it and hang on.

Ex's

I still miss my ex, but my aim is getting better.

Cheer Up

Someday you'll be dead.

Saints & Sinners

Every saint has a past, every sinner has a future.

Children

The softer you make it for your kids,
the harder their life will be.

Life

Life is wonderful, do your best not to miss it.

Salesman

That salesman could sell green
toothpaste to a man with no teeth.

Milk

Reindeer milk has five times the fat of cow's milk.

Women Want

Women want a man who's sensitive in
general and macho in life threatening situations.

Self Absorbed

He had a big heart tattooed on his arm
with the words below "I love me."

Trees

The southern branch feels the warmth of spring first.

Past

Once upon a time on the new year,
youth gave poems to Elders wishing them long life.

North Wind

The north wind is the spirit of the roaring Siberian Tiger.

Hell

The religion of Hell is patriotism and the
government is an enlightened democracy.
James Cabell

One Liners

Facts And Figures
Nothing is so fallacious as facts, except figures.
George Canning

Learning
Wise men learn more from fools than fools from wise men.
Marcus Cato

Enjoyment
Enjoy what is, before it isn't.

Women
All women are good, good for nothing
or good for something.
Miguel de Cervantes

Revitalize
Revitalize, balance hot and cold.

Love
In love, everything is true, everything is false, it is the
one subject of which one cannot express an absurdity.
Micholas Chamfort

Life
Life is creating, create what you want!!

Fertile Womb
A fertile womb is like a pomegranate.

The Bible Sez

The Bible tells us to love our neighbors, and also
to love our enemies; probably because
they are generally the same people.
Gilbert Chesteston

Pearls

The children of oysters and moonlight.

Cure For Vice

The cure for vice is long years of study
and practice, eventually the years cure it.

Religious Values

Religious values are seldom found
in religious people's actions.

Eggs

A hen is only an eggs way of making another egg.
Sammel Buller

Creating

We all create our own little hell.

Life

Life is mostly action resulting
in tiredness over and over again.

1917

Indian birth rate exceeds the death rate.

Cultured

A man should be just cultured enough to
be able to look with suspicion upon culture.
Sammel Butler

Humor

Humor is full of hidden truth.

Gross National Product

I don't want to increase the gross national product,
I want to increase the gross national happiness.
King Jigme Singye Wangchuck

The Sun

The Sun is the spirit of the east, of spring and new life.

Sin

Pleasures a sin, and sometimes sin's a pleasure.
George Byron.

World Population

The world population largely consists of two groups of
about equal numbers, the bores and the bored.

Wait

Wait long enough and everything will come, even death.

Pessimist

One who prides himself in seeing the worst
side of everything positive.

War

Behind ever war is the greed of those who gain.

Scientific Experiments

Substitute bureaucrats for animals in scientific experiments for further progress.

Cures

Death cures all diseases.

Truth

The naked truth doesn't offend nudists.

Young Writers

The young writers, are worth watching, not reading, just watching.
Dorothy Parker

Truth & Lies

Simple to tell the truth, difficult to lie well.

School Teachers

School teachers are so busy educating students that they don't have time to teach them anything.

Progress

Progress goes from one simple nuisance to another more complex nuisance.

Fools

Young men think old man are fools;
but old men know young men are fools.
George Chapman

Mankind

Mankind are very odd creatures; one half censure what
they practice, the other half practice what they censure.
Ben Franklin

Best Way

The best way out is always through.
Robert Frost

Quest For Truth

The terrible thing about the quest for truth is that you find it.
Renny de Gourmont

Staying In Bed

Don't stay in bed. . . unless you can make money in bed.
George Burns

Roosters And Hens

The rooster makes more racket than
the hen that lays the egg.
Joel Harris

Progress

Progress is continued advancement of
man's Material Gods.

Talking

Say only what you mean, mean only what you say.

Denial

Denial about alcohol and drugs is minuscule compared
to cultural denial; like a mosquito bite compared to a
nuclear bomb. Denial about the native,
indigenous people is even greater.

Good Families

Good families are generally worse than others.
Anthony Hope

Pollution Slogan

Give a hoot, don't pollute.

Fame

Fame is a fickle food, upon a shifting plate.
Emily Dickinson

Careful

You've got to be careful if you don't know where
you're going, because you might not get there.
Yogi Berra

Civilization

The human race is dying from civilization.

Faith

Say what you will about unquestioning faith.
I consider a capacity for it terrifying.
Kurt Vonnegut, Jr.

1917

Congress ends federal subsidies to Christian churches for Indian education.

Countdown Thoughts

Astronaut Alan Shepard's thoughts as he waited to be launched into space were "I just kept looking around me, remembering that everything in the capsule was supplied by the lowest bidder."

Legal

When the president does it, that means it is not illegal.
Richard Nixon

Idealism

Idealism is fine, but as it approaches reality, the cost becomes prohibitive.
William F. Buckley

Healing

Time heals and doctors get the money.

Kittens

Would you like a kitten, Sir? "No thanks, I just had lunch."

Fencin Trivia

It's harder to fence in
Goats & Hogs than
Cows & Horses

God Error

Believing that God is separate from you or anything else.

Arizona Sand Trout

Arizona Sand Trout burrow thru sand similar to their cousins swimming thru water. They are now believed extinct, the last known school of sand trout drowned in a flash flood in 1969.

Truth

Truth is the most valuable thing we have,
let us economize it.
Mark Twain

President Harry S. Truman

Harry was the first president to buzz
the White House in an airplane.

James Dean

Live fast, die young and leave a good looking corpse.

Rock Journalism

Most rock journalism is people who can't write interviewing people who can't talk for people who can't read.
Frank Zappa

Wisdom

A wise man may look ridiculous in the company of fools.

Taste

Simplicity is the background of good taste.

Temptation

The less the temptation, the greater the sin.

False American Myth

John F. Kennedy was a WWII hero when his tiny PT-109 patrol boat was rammed and sunk by a destroyer. Reality, Kennedy and most of the crew were asleep. They were caught off guard and rammed due to their negligence.

Success

If at first you don't succeed, try again.
Then quit. No use being a damn fool about it.
W.C. Fields

Names

A. Moron
Commissioner of Education in the Virgin Islands.

Cross Dressing In Space

In 1961 Bill Douglas became the first astronaut to enter space wearing women's lingerie.

Potato War

In 1943 a Navy ship was defended and saved by the crew throwing potatoes as the Japanese came topside, they thought the potatoes were hand grenades.

Right

I'm willing to admit that I may not always be right..
but I'm never wrong.
Samuel Goldwyn

Twins

In twenty percent of identical twins one is left handed.

Last Words

Black Jack Ketehum, before being hung said "I'll be in hell before you've finished breakfast boys.. let her rip."

Sex

Sex is one of the most beautiful
and natural things that money can buy.
Steve Martin

Doctor Translations

Let me schedule you for some tests, translates into,
I have a 40% interest in the lab.

Photographic Memories

Most everyone has a photographic memory but no film.

Politics: Word Origin

From the words "poly", meaning many, and
"ticks," as in small blood-sucking parasites.

Bad News

6 billion people, 1 billion at dangerously
high hormone levels of fertile reproductively.

Early Morning Choices

I can choose to be in a good mood or
I can choose to be in a bad mood.

Other People Complaining
I can accept their complaining or
I can point out the positive side of life.

Years
Where the hell do all the years go?

Close Trouble
Getting too close to someone before you know them.

Christian Charity
I think there is an immense shortage of
Christian Charity among so-called Christians.
Harry Truman

Prejudices
I hang on to my prejudices,
they are the testicles of my mind.
Eric Hoffer

Sea Cruise Marriages
Marriages performed by the captain are valid only for the
duration of the cruise.

Healthy Food And Exercise
Those who need 'em the most are those who avoid them.

Packaged Truth
Truth comes in packages of pain and light. Truth
denied makes our packages stranger and more painful.

Leaning
People can't let you down till after you've leaned on them.

Two Kinds Of People
Those who laugh and those who don't.

Humor
Humor is about perspective,
a willingness to address joy even in adversity.
C.W. Metcalf

Suffering
Suffering is one of our highly developed
skills that we don't need to use.

Long Time
It took a long time to learn not to trust people
who can't be trusted.

Co-Dependent Insurance
My fault insurance.

Willing Helpers
There are those willing to help you kill yourself and
there are those willing to help you heal yourself,
may you be willing to choose the latter.

Why
Don't ask why, ask why not!

Confucius Say

Confucius say, who say I say all
those things they say I say.

1917-18

World War I. Large numbers of Indians enlist, fight and die.

Taxes

A fine is a tax you pay for doing wrong and
a tax is a fine you pay for doing right.

Don't Wait

Someday you'll look back at this and laugh. Don't wait.

Names

Cardinal Sin,
Archbishop of Manila.

TV's Biggest Problem

TV's biggest problem is talking time between commercials.

Two Days Time

In two days tomorrow will be yesterday.

Enlightenment

Enlightenment is a firefly, not a flashlight.

Great Deeds

There are no great deeds,
only small deeds done with great love.
Mother Theresa

Permission

It's easier to ask for forgiveness than to ask for permission.

Bumper Sticker

Horn broken, watch for finger.

Divorce

A gift that lasts forever.

Perfume Names

The names of perfumes proves that
virtue doesn't make scents.

Shit Happens

Course in miracles: it's a miracle when shit happens.

Twelve step program: I admit I'm powerless over shit happening.

Economics: the rate of shit happening (in seasonally adjusted 1965 dollars) keeps getting worse.

Communism: shit happens because someone made a profit.

Psychoanalysis: Explaining why shit happens is anal.

New age: shit doesn't happen, if you experience the illusion of shit happening you need to learn something from it.

Sheldrake: once shit has happened, it happens again more easily.

Avatar: We create shit happening.

Missing Link

I believe I've found the missing
link between the animal and civilized man, it is us.
Dr. Konrad Lorenz

Temptation

Why resist temptation, there will always be more.
Don Herold

Dog

You can't call a dog honest if the meat is out of reach.

Whites Told

The whites told only one side.
Told it to please themselves. Told much that is not true.
Yellow Wolf, Nez Perce

Religion

Men never do evil so completely and cheerfully as
when they do it from religious conviction.
Blaire Pascal

Loving Women

A transsexual loves women so much he wants to join them.
Dr. Renee Richards

Books

Books can only tell you where another mind has been.

Retirement Problem

The problem with retirement is that you can't leave
all your problems at the office.

Self-Image

All the wonders you seek are within yourself.
Sir Thomas Browne

Statistics

Statistics are like ladies of the night.
Once you get them down, you can do anything with them.
Mark Twain

1918

The Native American Church is incorporated in Oklahoma.

Success-Happiness

Success is getting what you want,
happiness is wanting what you get.

Teaching

Nothing that is worth knowing can be taught.
Oscar Wilde

Difficulties

Difficulties of life are intended to make us better, not bitter.

Maturity

Acting your age instead of your urge.

Old

You're old when you have no enthusiasm.

Words

The ten commandment contain 297 words.
A federal directive to regulate the price of
cabbage contains 26,911 words.

Wages

It isn't the employer who pays the wages, he only handles the money. It is the product that pays the wages.
Henry Ford

Changing

Remember how hard it is to change yourself and how much harder it is to change others.

Opposition

Great spirits have always encountered violent opposition from mediocre minds.
Albert Einstein

Republican / Democratic

Republican government: Man exploits Man
Democratic government: Just reversed

Missing Church

Sorry I missed church, I've been busy practicing witchcraft and becoming a lesbian.

God Laugh

If you want to hear God laugh tell him your plans.

A Dog's Love

Even a dog's love is hard to understand.

My Grave

Don't cry over my grave, I'm not there, take a deep breath of fresh air for that is now me.

Sortin Beans
Even the poorest of the poor, sort their beans.

Advantage
Any animal, including humans
has an advantage in their home area.

Wild Ones
The wild ones are the only ones worth havin.

Arizona Extremes
Arizona has had both the nations daily high temperature
and the nations low temperature.

Words
My words are like the stars that don't change.
Seattle

Religion
If you want a country run by religion, move to Iran.

President Herbert Hoover
Hoover was the first president to have
an asteroid named after him

Don't
Don't smoke, Don't drink & Don't do drugs.

Wisdom
He that is a wise man by day is a fool by night.

Church Bulletin

For those of you who have children and don't know it,
we have a nursery downstairs.

Do

Ride bicycles.

Publishing

In the 1930's Dr. Seuss was turned down by 27 publishers.
The excuse I got for all those rejections was that there was
nothing on the market quite like it, so they didn't know
whether it would sell.
Dr. Seuss

Will

Write a living will.

Religion

We have just enough religion to makes us hate but not
enough to make us love one another.
Jonathon Swift

Bills

Keep your bills minimal & pay them promptly.

Regret

My one regret in life is that I'm not someone else.
Woody Allen

Life

Life is a foreign language: all men mispronounce it.
Christopher Morley

Eloguence

Eloguence flourished most in Rome when
public affairs were in the worst condition.
Michael Montaigne

Take Time

Take time to smell the flowers.

Travelers

We're all travelers on this road of life,
unsure of our distination and arrival time.

Hard

The idea that there is some hard reality that we have to
adapt ourselves to and be realistic about is just another
form of fear.
Harry Palmer

Pray

Pray for guidance, wisdom and courage.

Critics

Don't respond to your critics.

Two Kinds Of People

There are two kinds of people in the world, those that let
their pets (livestock) in the house and those that don't.

Movie Quotes

Six of the top ten movie quotes are
from the 1930's and 40's.

Choice
There was a time when I had a choice...
Red Eagle

Negativity
Avoid negative people.

Respect
Show respect for all things.

Your Church
What can your church do for me, that God can't do?

Winning
Be willing to lose a battle to win the war.

Overnight Success
Overnight success usually takes many years.

New Ways
Be open to new ways.

Tough
The meat was so tough, had to sharpen
the knife just to cut the gravy.

Impressions
You never get a second chance
to make a good first impression.

Problems

Big problems disguise big opportunities.

Museums

Museums house specimens, now lifeless.

Keys

Hide an extra key to your home &
vehicle to prevent lock out.

Fool

Making a fool of yourself is easy but not permanent.

Giving

You can give without love
but you can't love without giving.

Man / Woman

Woman - Do you love me still?
Man - Yes, better than any other way.

On Listening

Listen! or your tongue will make you deaf.
Cherokee Saying

Two Or More

People come together who have many faults in common.

Alcoholics

Alcoholics are more likely to wear sunglasses
on dark days or at nite.

Understanding
To understand is to pardon.

Nebraska Ag Producers
10/98 Nebraska rural development commission estimates
that 10,000 out of 55,000 ag producers will go
out of business in the next two years.

1924
Citizenship granted to all America Indians.

Dogs
Dogs are lovable because their tails
wag instead of their tongues.

Friend
A friend comes when other don't.

Mirror
This morning I looked in that mirror, and saw,
a reverse before and after picture.

Cigarette Smoking
Cigarette smoking is the largest
cause of premature death in the USA.

Topeka, KS Law
No alcohol in a teacup.

Pray For The Best
Pray for the best, prepare for the worst, and
remember that the outcome ain't up to you.

Lost Moment

Lost it in a moment of fear and stupidity.

Books

Books average 400 words per page.

Children & Dogs

Anyone who hates children and dogs can't be all bad.
W.C. Fields

Suspects

Negroes, Mexicans, Orientals and Indians
are suspected of everything except being white.

Up The Ladder

No matter how high up the ladder you get
someone can bring you down.

Successful

Many are successful due to more determination, than talent.

Cure For Hypochondria

Gene Weingarter discovered the cure
for hypochondria is getting sick.

Arkansas

Arkansas has the highest divorce rate.

Skin Disease

The earth has a skin and that skin has skin
diseases; one of its diseases is called man.
Freidrich Wilhelm

One Liners

Forgiveness

Everyone has need to be forgiven.

Sinners

Only the sinner has a right to preach.
Christopher Morley

Goals

Everybody sets out to do something, and everybody does
something, but no one does what he sets out to do.
George Moore

Classified

Handyman will do anything your husband won't.

Oprah

Oprah Winfrey is the most powerful
person in show business.

American Meals

If we now consider typical American meals with a
critical eye, we see innocent stupidity elevated to an art.
Adelle Davis

Life

Do what you will, this life's a fiction,
and is made up of contradiction.
William Blake

Losing

When you lose, the world does not come to an end.
Bruno Bettelheim

Shortest Way

The shortest way to do many things is to
do only one thing at once.
Samuel Smiles

Indians & Time

Indians were time rich.
Tom Brown Jr.

Kindness

Planting kindness and harvesting love.

Love

You can't waste love.

Stories

I am always at a loss to know how
much to believe of my own stories.
Washington Irving

Children

Children should be seen and not had.

Mother's Voice

It's very hard to hear my mother's voice coming out of me.
Whoopi Goldberg

Speed

There is more to life than increasing its speed.
Gandhi

Parent

If you have never been hated by your child,
you have never been a parent.
Bette Davis

Flowers

Some of the thorniest flowers have the sweetest scent.

Love

Love: a season's pass on the shuttle
between heaven and hell.
Don Dickerman

Dance

Dance the upward spiral dance.

Fate

There's a divinity that shapes our ends
rough - helm them how we will.
Shakespeare

Reverse Side

The reverse side also has a reverse side.
Japanese Proverb

Grateful

I'm grateful that the outcomes are out of my control.

Life Forms

Life forms feed on each other, or
more accurately feed each other.

Friend

You want a friend in this life, get a dog.
Harry Truman

Only A Fool

Only a fool thinks you can't joke and be serious.

Started Out With Nothing

The old retired farmer / rancher had started
out with nothing and still had most of it left.

Gospel, Blues Difference

In gospel it's "Lordy-Lordy" In blues it's "Baby-Baby".

Ultimate Compliment

The ultimate compliment to a musician and / or singer is:
That usta be my favorite song.

Average Wedding?

The average wedding now costs $19,000?

Clinton

I didn't ask her to lie on the disposition,
but I did ask her to lie in a different position.

Women & Life

There ain't no free rides.

Opinions

Don't let your opinions sway your judgement.
Samuel Goldwyn

Sacred
Sacred is ordinary - Ordinary is sacred

Judgement
Judgement determines whether its a weed or a flower.

Clark Gable
Clark Gable's first screen test was a failure
because they thought his ears were to big.

Scars
Scars hold the memory of pain.

Starving Child
A starving child wants only to eat.

Brains
Why were men given larger brains than dogs?
So they won't hump women's legs at parties.

1928
The Meriam Report deplores Indian conditions
and declares the allotment system a failure.

Words
The words in the poem washed over me like forever.

More Jobs?
I'd prefer less people to more jobs.

Six Word History Lesson
What was, isn't. What is, wasn't.

Camp
Camp Poison Ivy.

Money
About 2/3 of the money that puts people
in federal office comes from big corporations.

Teachers
You can't step into your teacher's shoes.

Before The Fad
Before the fad of laying in the sun to get a tan we worked
outside and would take a break and lay in the shade.

Greyhound Therapy
Buy 'em a one way ticket.

Seven Deadly Sins
7 deadly sins, created, categorized &
described for your weakly enjoyment.

In Life
In life there are more fizzlers than sizzlers.

Everything Is Two Ways
Everything is two ways, the way it's suppose
to be and the way it is.

Beginnings
Beginnings are more fun than endings.

You Can't Be Stronger
You can't be stronger than your destiny.

Sex
The young go a long way for a little sex and
a little sex goes a long way for the old.

1926
National council of American Indians is founded.

Deer Hunters
Deer hunters are proof that a deer keeps
getting bigger after it is killed.

Down / Up
Down on the farm, up on the ranch.

Fear
To him who is in fear everything rustles.
Sophocles

Friends
Fate makes our relatives, choice makes our friends.
Jacques Delille

Restful Vacation
Stay at home and rest for your vacation.

Future

Shallow men speak of the past;
wise men of the present; and fools of the future.
Mane der Deffand

Famous Inventor

For many years he worked & worked, he was called
a crackpot and a fool, with his efforts he hit the jackpot,
and is now called a genius.

Remember the Alamo

Remember the Alamo, order pie ala mode.

Keep On

Just keep on truckin.

Machoism

It is good to know, that machoism, is alive and
well. Well... Sick in Nebraska.

Desire

A man wants to satisfy desire.
A women wants only to desire.

Assumption Accuracy

Assumptions: usually off about 180 degrees.

Extreme Measures

Man is the only land animal that goes to such
extremes measures to shit in the water.

Superficial
People are easily attracted by the superficial.

Artless
The artless are usually in charge of running the arts.

Hollywood DT's
I've been asked if I ever get the DT's, I don't know.
It's hard to tell where Hollywood ends and the DT's begin.
W.C. Fields

Traveling
Positive change requires traveling the long
distance from left brain to right brain.

Winners / Losers
Winners never remember, losers never forget.

Simple
Keep it simple.

Gettin By
You might get by with it but you won't get away with it.

Jesus
Jesus has been reincarnated, lives in Mississippi, weights
275#, is single, black and she has seven daughters.

1930
Senate survey disclaims BIA kidnapping of Indian children.

Very Hard Work

I've done a lot of very hard work for a long,
long time to become ordinary.
Barbara Van Cleve

Taste

Rolls Royce taste with a junky old Ford pocketbook.

Civilizing The Natives

Providing money to natives that didn't need it before the
invaders came.

Auto Repair

The end of April is the slowest time in the auto
repair business. Best time to get work done.

Perceiving

Become open to perceiving that which you
haven't been able to perceive.

When I Grow Up

When I Grow Up, I want to be -- a child.

Humans

We humans are animals with laughter and tears.

Perfectionism

Become more human.

Over And Over

Do it, over and over, as many times as it is necessary.

Pleasure
Don't chase pleasure so fast that you miss it.

Assumption
Assumption is the mother of screw up.
Angelo Denghia

Power
Power corrupts and absolute power corrupts absolutely.
Lord Actores Thesis

Problems
Problems return even larger when ignored.

Peace
Make peace with yourself first.

Animal Shows
Animal shows - the more nervous the person showing
the animal, the more nervous the animal.

Investment Speculation
There are two times in a man's life when he should not
speculate: when he can't afford it and when he can.
Mark Twain

Harvest
We can only harvest what we plant.

Writers
Writers rewrite.

Most Popular Business
The most popular business is definitely monkey business.

Season
Each season provides for the season that follows.

Simplicity
Simplicity is more valuable than complexity.

Most Dangerous Animal
The most dangerous animal is man.

1934
US Indian Reorganization Act (IRA)
reverses US policy of allotment.

Snow
Snow is wonderful, it makes everyone's yard look the same

Freedom
Is your freedom limited by the opinions of others?

Needs
What the country needs is dirtier fingernails
and cleaner minds.
Will Rogers

Misfortune
The worst misfortune that can happen to an
ordinary man is to have an extraordinary father.
Austin O'Malley

Creativity and Talent

Creativity and talent require action to be of value.

Examples

One person living it, is better than 10 preaching it.

Telling The Truth

He who tells the truth doesn't sin,
but he causes many inconveniences.

Before You Tie

See before you tie, know how you can untie.

Speaking

Let not the tongue speak what the head
may have to pay for.

Retaliating

If you return an ass's kicks, most of the pain is yours.

The Rat

The rat that knows but one hole is soon caught by the cat.

Love

Love flies away and the pain remains.

Federal Aid Explained

Giving yourself a blood transfusion by
drawing blood out of your left arm, returning it to you right
arm, and spilling 90% on the way.

Said & Done

There is a great distance between said and done.

Taste

Half an orange tastes as sweet as a whole one.

Cowboy / Cattleman

A cowboy has a big buckle over his belly;
a cattleman has a big belly over his buckle.

Get A Grip

If you want to get a grip on things, look for the handle.

Wine & Whining

Wine & whining won't bring happiness.

Marriage

Most marriages don't add two people together.
They subtract one from the other.
James Bond

Christian Rule #1

Christian Rule #1 is don't look or act like Christ.

Violence

Violence is as American as cherry pie.
Stockely Carmichael

Refuses

When one refuses, two cannot quarrel.

Flop

The only thing that's been a worse flop than
the organization of nonviolence has been,
is the organization of violence.
Joan Baez

Marriage

Marriage is a great way to spend a weekend.

Cooties & Fleas

Cooties graze and bed down but a flea ain't never satisfied.

Quiet

He was quieter than a post hole.

1939

The Seneca issue a declaration of
independence from the state of New York.

Men

You've never know a man until you have divorced him.
Zsa Zsa Gabor

Cold

Cold'ern a bankers smile.

Narrow Minded

He was so narrow minded, could look thru a keyhole
with both eyes at the same time.

Corkscrew

A corkscrew never pulled a man out of a hole.

Anger

When right we can afford to keep our tempers,
when wrong we can't afford not to.

City Dude

City Dude, never closer to a cow than a glass of milk.

Safer

Sometimes safer to pull your freight than your gun.

Female Hollywood Diet

Three males a day.

Time

If you can't get the job done in five shots,
then it's time to get the hell out of there.

Belief

Belief is a disease.
Werner Erhart

Nothin

Nothin under his hat but hair.

Aigs

Do you want your aigs bright-eyed or dirty on both sides?

Toughest
He was the toughest man west of anyplace east.

Happy
Happy as a pig eatin coal.

Mouths
The bigger the mouth the better it looks shut.

Repenting
If I repent of anything, it is likely to be my good behavior.
Henry David Thoreau

Hot Words
Hot words lead to cold slabs.

Fast Horse
Had a horse so fast it's shadow couldn't keep up.

Home
It's as hard to get a man to stay home
after you've married him as it was to get him to
go home before you married him.
Helen Rowland

Hot
It got so hot that summer that the hens
laid hard boiled eggs.

New York City Dogs
New York City dogs produce 20,000 tons
of excretement per year.

Burrocrats

Burrocrats would make a good free lunch for coyotes.

Drowning

Nobody ever drowned in their own sweat.

Virtue

Virtue is insufficient temptation.
George Bernard Shaw

Lazy

He was too lazy to even smile.

Cows & Bulls

You need 1 bull for 25 cows.

Blood

Blood boils without flame.

Stories

Always tell your stories wider than tall.

1944

National Congress of America Indians is organized.

Campaign Advice

Always campaign against the truth.

Blushing

Man is the only animal that blushes, or needs to.
Mark Twain

False American Myth

General Douglas Mac Arthur is credited with the quote, "old soldiers never die; they just fade away." Reality, He took the line from a WWI British Army song.

Sanity

Sanity is a matter of degree.
Aldous Huxley

Bad

He was so bad the buzzards couldn't stomach him.

Creativity

Creativity is neither the product of neurosis or simple talent, but an intense courageous encounter with the Gods.
Rollo May

His Potential

His mother was a whore & his father was old man trouble.

Friends

Had more friends than there are fiddlers in Hell.

Bad Luck

A good run of bad luck can be some good medicine to make you change your ways.

Rain

Rain enough to drown ducks.

Cowboy Fears

Cowboys are afraid of decent women & being left afoot.

Hen Pecked

He was so hen-pecked he moulted every year.

Truth

There's a difference in truth & truth by products.

Phoenix Sun

There's so much sun in Phoenix that during the heat of summer the sundials run a half hour fast.

Flies

Flies bite more before it rains.

Names

Major Minor, an officer in the U.S. Army.

Advice

Call airlines, trains and buses to be sure they're on time before leaving to meet one.

Prayer: Civilized / Native

The civilized pray with their palms together. The native pray with their arms wide, palms holding the universe.

Four Seasons In Phoenix

The four season in Phoenix, Spring: long & beautiful.
Summer: longer than spring & hotter than hell.
Fall: 2 days between Thanksgiving & Christmas.
Winter: 2 months with some frosts after the fall.

Goals

Wellness, fitness, & balance.

Seeking

Most folks seek the illusion of security
while avoiding opportunity.

Family

Don't get married unless you want to start raising
a family, and don't start raising a family unless
you want to get married.
R.A. Lyman

Nixon

I would have made a good pope.
Richard Nixon

Daylight Savings Time

Arizona does not have daylight savings time.
Any desert rat knows they can't stand anymore
daylight in the summer heat.

James Dean

James Dean avoided the draft by
registering as a homosexual.

Temptations

There are terrible temptations which
requires strength and courage to yield to.
Oscar Wilde

Children & Pets

Another good thing about pets & children is they
seldom drag out pictures of their owners.

Unimportant

It's impossible to over exaggerate the unimportantance of everything.

Change

The metal bands on migratory birds are used to record information for the Washington biological Survey abbreviation on the tags reads WASH BIOL SURV.
A letter included the statement: while camping last week I shot one of your birds. I think it was a crow.
I followed the cooking instructions on the leg tag and I want to tell you, it was horrible -- the bands are now marked "FGWS" for Fish and Games, Wildlife Service.

Security

Security is mostly illusion.

Truth

Solomon could honestly tell a bride that she was one woman in a thousand.

Cows

Momma cows ain't no ladys.

Judge Roy Bean

Judge Roy Bean fined a corpse. $40 (the $ in his pockets) for carrying a concealed weapon.

Age

Women don't admit their age and men don't act theirs.

Senior Citizens Aids

Hearing aids, band aids, walking aids, roll aids,
seeing aids, medical aids, government aids,
and monetary aids for children and grandchildren.

Fear

Most folks are more afraid of life than death.

Doctor Translations

You need to make another appointment for next week,
translates to I can make more money
by charging you for another office visit.

Creating

You want to be responsible for creating yourself,
not just for getting to a point where you can live
with yourself. You're creators. You're not adjusters.
Harry Palmer

Meetings

For maximum productivity limit a meeting
to a maximum of four people.

Experience

No one knows what he can do till he tries.
Publilius Syrus

Road Kill Dogs

Twenty percent of the dog population is
killed yearly by vehicles.

Painting A Car To Sell
Very dark for luxury, red or bright yellow for sporty,
cheaper paint & body work look best white,
green is the hardest to sell.

Looks
Looked like he'd crawled thur a
bob wire fence at ninety miles per hour.

Ice
Blue ice is safer to walk on then black ice.

1941-45
World War II, over 25,000 Indians serve active duty,
thousands work in war related industry.

Recovery
It takes ten years to recover from heavy use of LSD.

Roadkill
Nearly half of the deer hit by vehicles are
struck in May & November.

Seattle
There was a time when our people covered
the land as the waves of a wind-ruffled sea...
that time long since passed... I will not mourn...
Seattle

Life
Life is kinda like squeezing laughter from an onion.

Two Birds Together

Tie two birds together. They will not be able to fly,
even thou they now have four wings.
Jalaludin Rumi, Sufi

Yawning

Schizophrenics very seldom yawn.

Chickens / Rain

Chickens run for cover before a brief shower
but stay out for a long rain.

Wisdom

Wisdom is gained from the pain of experience.

Hallucination

Auditory hallucinations indicate mental illness,
other hallucinations indicate physical illness.

Tobacco Addicts

Tobacco addicts seldom quit on their first attempt.

Fat Test

Too much fat in your diet makes your turds float.

Love

Love is strong as death.
Song of Solomon

Smokers & Drinkers

Smokers & drinkers usually start before age twenty-five.

Fluorescent Light

It takes about as much energy to start up a
fluorescent light as to run it one hour.

Crime

The crime rate goes down in bad weather.

Snakes

Red next to yellow can kill a fellow.
Red next to black is a friend of jack.

Driving

Little is gained by changing lanes in heavy traffic.

Art

There are moments when art attains dignity
almost to the dignity of manual labor.
Oscar Wilde

Eyes

Eyes to the front - carnivorous.
Eyes to the side - vegetarian.

Meat

The meat of one elephant equals that
of one hundred antelope.

Red

The color red gets the most attention.

Roadside Magazines
Two-thirds of magazines thrown along roadsides
will be pornographic.

Fresh Fish
Fresh fish has eyes that are clean, bulging & shiny.

Complainers
In any organization the one who
complains the most does the least.

Right Prices
On ounce of gold equals 13 barrels of oil.

Spreading The Word
TV, radio, newspaper advertising plus posters will inform
about half the people, the rest are informed by word of
mouth. About twenty percent won't be informed.

Rat Hole
A full grown rat can go thru a hole the size of a quarter.

Mount Everest.
One out of eight die climbing to the top of Mount Everest.

Child Development
Your child will become as you describe the child to others.

1941-45
Some Indians are jailed as draft resisters.

Vietnam Bombs

During the Vietnam War over 3 million bombs per year, each leaving a crater 20-30' deep and 30-40' in diameter.

Drugs

Caffeine highs last about four hours.

Bull Definition

A Bull is a male cow that is roped in Arizona, rode in U.S. rodeos, fought in Mexico and shot in Washington D.C.

Three Types Of Non Paying Renters

Those who wish to pay but can't, Those who can but won't, Those who can't and wouldn't if they could.

Intellect And Learning

Stop boasting of intellect and learning;
for here intellect is hampering, and learning is stupidity.
Hakin Jami, Sufi

Divorce

A baby born today has an 80% chance of being the victim of a divorce by age 15, and another 80% chance of their own divorce by age 30.

Water

Half your body weight in pounds is the number of ounces of water you need to drink daily.

Crime

Commit a federal crime you're less likely to go to jail and if you do they are nicer.

Snow

An average snow of ten inches equals one inch of rain.

Colds

Begin a new job and come down with a cold in ten days.

Obeying

The white man does not obey the Great Spirit,
that is why the Indian can't agree with him.
Flying Hawk

Stories

Stories only happen to people who can tell them.

Deeper Need

Listen to that deeper need that is
inside you and celebrate filling it.

Meeting Room

A comfortable meeting room requires
30 square feet per person.

Recovery

It takes over a week to get over a day in a hospital

Franklin, Nebraska

Planks - Plunk and Bunk Motel

Education

I have never let my schooling interfere with my education.
Mark Twain

Roam

I want to roam the prairies. There I am free and happy.
Santana

Tornado Bait

Mobile home parks.

Cold Feet

Cold feet are not cool.

Snow

Near or below zero, walking on snow
makes a squeaking sound.

Corn

Two bushel of ear corn equals one bushel of shelled corn.

Driving

To avoid getting pulled over drive the
same speed as everyone else.

Water

Clear water is about twice as deep as it looks.

World Of Finance

It's hard to recover from being in the world of finance.

Shoplifters

1 out of 50 people in a store are shoplifters.
1 out of 200 get caught.

Meetings

A meeting with a followed agenda accomplishes
twice as much in half the time.

Money / Karma

Can you make more money than Karma?

Fencing

Stolen property brings 10% of what the
item would sell for if not stolen.

Day Off

50% of those who call in sick are actually sick
because you can't call in well to get out of work.

Planting

Plant root crops at full moon and
above ground crops at new moon.

Direction

Dead tree directions - wet under the bark on the north side.

Troubled Children

Troubled children mutter under their breath steadily.

Speak

Speak to everyone in accordance with his understanding.
Sufi

In The Name Of Religion

Many fatten themselves in the name of religion.

Crick Water

That crick water was so thick you could plow it.

Longevity

Self employed people live longer.

Hugs

Four hugs a day are minimum.

Arizona Fact

In Arizona, you can't fry an egg on the sidewalk when its 120^0, but you can on a black car hood, but it ruins the paint.

Nuts

Brazil nuts are the most radioactive food.

Jobs

Eighty percent of the jobs require less
than eight months training.

Fool

He was a fool before meeting her
she just shined a lite on it.

Debt

The best thing to do with debt is to prevent and eliminate it.

Working

Working a horse or mule hard all day, requires 3 quarts of
grain morning & nite and 10 pounds of hay a day.

Height

Shorter people live longer and have less back trouble.

He Don't Exactly Lie

He just rearranges the truth in his favor.

Favors

A busy person is most likely to do a favor.

Creation

Why did God make men before women?
You need a rough draft before you make a final copy.

Clothes

Don't wear clothes that have more character than you do.

College

Succeeding in college - avoid young
and elderly professors.

1941-45

Navajo marines become famous for using
their language as the battlefield code.

Meat

Cook Meat for one half hour at 350⁰ per pound.

New York

The New York City rat population
equals the people population.

Vietnam Herbicides

During the Vietnam War close to 10 million acres
were sprayed with Agent Orange / Agent White,
including the last virgin tropical forest.

Treatment

Treat everyone like you want to be treated.

Ten Bears

I know every stream and every wood...
like my fathers before me, I live happily.
Ten Bears

Divorce

The chances of divorce are greatest
during the fourth year of marriage.

Joy

Live joyfully today.

Last Words

Chris Hubback, who shot herself while broadcasting
the news, "and now, in keeping with channel 40's
policy of always bringing you the latest in blood and guts,
in living color, you're about to see another first,
an attempted suicide."

Lying

A used car salesman knows when he's lying,
most other salesman don't.

Secrets
Don't divulge secrets.

Recovery
Recovering form the death of a
spouse is hard, divorce is harder.

Short Prayer
If your parachute doesn't open limit your last prayer to
15 seconds as that's about the length of life left.

Writing
If a 6th grader can't understand it, rewrite it so he can.

Husbands
Husbands are like wood fires,
when unattended, they go out.

Green Lights
Speeding 5-10 MPH increases the
number of green lights you can make.

Comparison
Compare 25,000 years use by native Americans
to 500 years by Europeans.

Coon Weather
Raccoons eat heavily 48 hours before a major winter snow.

Feeding Dogs
One pound of dry dog food for thirty pounds of dogs.

Guilt

Christians feel guilty for what they weren't allowed
to do and did. Jews feel guilty for what they
were supposed to do but didn't.

Prejudices

It is never too late to give up our prejudices.
Thoreau

Postage

An envelope with five sheets of paper will
go for a standard single stamp.

Weather Change

Prevailing weather is more likely to change three days
before a new moon and a full moon.

Interference

Don't let your brain interfere with your heart.

Parking Meter Income

The income from city parking meters is abut half the
income fines, from expired parking meters.

Food Test

Food that's normally hard is bad when it's turned soft and
vice versa.

Men / Women

Women think a man will change,
men think a woman won't change,
they're both wrong.

Farming

The farmer works the soil, the agriculturist works the farmer.
E.F. Ware

Do

Do smile a lot.

Divorce / Marriage

Getting divorced just because you don't love a man
is almost as silly as getting married just because you do.
Zsa Zsa Gabor

Don't

Don't swear.

Black Powder

The amount of black powder it takes to cover the
ball when held in the hollow of your palm is
about right for a muzzle loading rifle.

Time

No one can pass into eternity; we are already in it.

1900 Lower Middle-Class

In 1900 census takers marked any family with
2 servants or less as lower middle-class.

Sky

A curdy sky never leaves the ground dry.

Nails & Screws
a nail or screw needs to be 2-3 times longer
than the thickness you're attaching.

Heart
An elephant has a bushel basket size heart.

China Agriculture Commune Lesson
Human waste is collected, allowed to ferment 2-3 months
in an air tight concrete tank. It is then odorless and
disease-free and is used as fertilizer on vegetable plots.

Soybeans
On pound of soybeans makes two
and a half pounds of tofu.

Repairing
If an item costs under $100
it ain't worth paying anyone to fix.

Safe Predictions
Predicting the future - predict what but never when.

Cirrus Clouds
Weather will change after you see cirrus clouds.

Studs
Electrical outlets are usually attached
to the right hand side of a stud.

Writing

Write one thought per sentence.

Man

Man is nature's sole mistake.
William Gilbert

Freedom

Become debt free.

Injuries

For musculoskeletal injuries use ice
on new injuries and heat on old ones.

Appearances

Simple things are more complex that they appear.
Complex things are more simple than they appear.

Dull Knife

His knife was so dull, had to heat it up some to cut butter.

Mileage

Shoes are good for a 1000 miles, bicycle tires are good
for 4000 miles, car tires are good for 20-60,000 miles.

Life

Life is what happens to you while
you're making other plans.

Clothing

When in doubt wear bright colors.

Dressing
I dress for women and I undress for men.
Angie Dickinson

Church Bulletin
The low self-esteem support group will meet
Thursday at 7 p.m., please use the back door.

Life's Purpose
It all has a purpose, if not, what a waste.

What Man Really Knows
Men suppose, fancifully, that they know truth
and divine perception. In fact, they know nothing.
Juzjani, Sufi

Protein
1 Pound of grasshoppers = 3 pounds of beef

One Third
One third of Americans are unable to snap their fingers.

Two Men
When choosing between two males,
I always like to take the one I'ver never tried before.
Mae West

Success
Success is focusing on the solution to the problem.

Honesty

There are honest journalists
like there are honest politicians.
When bought, they stay bought.
Bill Moyers

Sales Tool

The most powerful sales tool is silence.

Pool Sign

Pool is open 24 hours a day,
please don't enter at any other time.

Wisdom

Some are wise, and some are otherwise.

Hollywood Marriages

In Hollywood all marriages are happy. It's trying to live
together afterwards that causes problems.
Shelley Winters

Talkers Defined

A gossiper talks about others, a bore talks about himself,
great conversationalists talks to you about you.

1946

The policy of "termination" goes into effect
with intention of ending special Indian trust status.

Newspaper

A newspaper is the lowest thing there is.
Mayor Richard Daley

News

I can get a better grasp of what is going on in the world
from one good Washington dinner party than from all
the background information NBC piles on my desk.
Barbara Walters

Quiet

Quiet as a stone wall.

Hollywood

Hollywood's a place where they'll pay you a thousand
dollars for a kiss, and fifty cents for your soul.
Marilyn Monroe

Disbelief

He was a believer in disbelief.

Horse Show

Horses' asses showing Horses' asses to Horses' asses

Knees

The elephant is the only animal with four knees.

Faces Of The Past

The faces of the past are like leaves that settle to
the ground... they make the Earth rich and thick,
so that nice fruit will come forth every summer.
Chief Dan George

Sorrow

Sorrow swims and grows big & fat in alcohol.

Goals

The most important goals are those that excite you.

Sex Appeal

Sex appeal is 50% what you've got and
50% what people think you've got.
Sophia Loren

Time

Time is the great equalizer

Health

Every day you do one of two things:
build health or produce disease in yourself.
Adelle Davis

Humor

The biggest laughs are based on the
biggest disappointments and the biggest fears.
Kurt Vonnegut, Jr.

Love Of Mothers

There is no love like that of most mothers.

Sense

I have a sixth sense, not the other five.
If I wasn't making money they'd put me away.
Red Skelton

Modern Man

Modern man is now responsible for the greatest number of
extinction of species in history.

Advice

Don't ask for advice when you already know the answer.

Women

Plain women know more about men
than beautiful ones do.
Katherine Hepburn

Curved Line

A curved line in the loveliest distance between two points.
Mae West

Windy Friend

Windy Friend: Blows & goes, means well, but tests
everyone's patience, like the Nebraska wind.

Arguing

Why do you want to be the other half of an argument?

Why?

Why do you take by force what you could obtain by love?
Powhatan

Attitude

Change your attitude and the world changes.

Freedom

The only freedom too many believe in is
"Freedom from personal responsibility."

Road To Drugs

The road to the drug world is paved with alcohol.

Sleeping With Dogs

If you sleep with dogs, you're gonna get fleas.

Real Cowboy

Three cowboys in a pickup, which one is the real cowboy?
The one on the left is a truck driver. The one on the right
is a gate opener. The one in the middle is a
"real cowboy" as he does nothin.

Around

What goes around comes around.

Problems

Most of the problems today wouldn't exist if those
Europeans had come to learn & change
instead of to conquer & convert.

Growing

Growing always comes with growing pains.

Illegal Drugs

People doin illegal drugs don't
make me breathe their smoke.

Christians

Christians - most hateful, ruthless group of people on the
face of the Earth. Wherever there are white people,
there is Christianity and there are missionaries.
They send the Christian missionaries in first
to preach turn-the-other-check, then they come
with their armies to conquer the people.
Nathan McCall

Sinners

The worst sinners make the best saints.

Struggle

Olive Oatman was captured by Apaches and
recaptured by anglos years later. Her desperate
struggle to get back to her Indian husband and children
shook many peoples belief in civilization.

Overstress

Overstress, and then, regress and that's the way it is.

Food Advice

Eat cheap food because
the products you excrete are of low value.

No, I Ain't Deaf

The motel manager just called to ask me to turn down
the TV cause them folks next door got overly sensitive ears.

Poetic Fact

Poets making points, have to use a fact now & then.

The Law

The law is merely an instrument to sanctify the
crimes of the powerful and to suppress
the aspirations of the less privileged.
Michael Andrews

Picture Takin Advice

When things are goin to Hell, don't stop to take pictures.

Cheap
He was so cheap that he squeezed the Buffalo on a nickel
till it shit a dime, then bitched cause it wasn't a quarter.

Real Farmer
You might be a real farmer if you've never bought a cap.

Swimming
A Beaver can hold its breath for 15 minutes
and swim underwater for half a mile!

Simple
Simple pleasures are the last refuge of the complex.
Oscar Wilde

Road Map
Lots of alcohol and/or drugs will turn
your skin into a road map to Hell.

Tobacco & Milk
Tobacco is not addictive but too much
milk might be bad for us.
1996 presidential candidate Dole

Annoying Ecologists
Ecologists are annoying in that they are usually right.

Love & Hate
When love swells, hate shrinks.

Perseverance VS Intelligence

Perseverance will overcome intelligence every time,
and I'm going to stick to it.
Alabama Representative Don Young

Messiahs

Live messiahs are dangerous to the established order
and are killed in the name of god & country.

Potential Great Poet

Could'a been great if it wasn't for
too much money, education & prestige.

Love

Love don't knock when it comes.

Smart, Smarter, Smartest

Smart - Knows it's all B.S., Smarter - Accepts it all anyhow,
Smartest - Loves it all anyhow.

Christ

Jesus Christ was not a Christian.

1946

U.S. Indian claims commission is created by
congress to settle tribal land claims against the U.S.

Optimists / Pessimists

The optimist proclaims that we live in the best of all
possible worlds, and the pessimists fears this is true.
James Cabell

Hollywood Progress

Today there are more Hollywood gun owners
in the closet than homosexuals.

Following

Following another's path leads to who they are,
not to who you are. You have to make this journey yourself.
Avatar teaches the use of proven navigational tools that
can be used, in harmony with one's own integrity, to pass
sagely across the uncharted turbulence of the
mind into the region of the soul.
Harry Palmer

Optimistic Hope For The Future

Prayin that no one shows up for the next war.

Final Birthday Gift

After death you don't have any more birthdays.

Sick

Been lickin outa the pan of misery too long.

Fare Fear

Taxis plan to raise the fare,
but we have nothing to fear but fare itself.

Luxuries

Anyone can afford expensive dreams.

Helpful Household Hint

Need a strainer? Can't find one? Use the fly swatter.

Ladder Advice
For Those Afraid Of Heights

Always use ladders in the horizontal position.
Never use a ladder in the vertical position.

Ex's Hated

Ex's hate their ex's usually because,
they know too much about them.

Nature

Nature would be better off if people quite playing God.

Politicians

Politicians are like children playing with matches -
can't comprehend the damage they may cause.

Business Sign

Employees, Agents and Representatives of City,
County, State and Federal Government agencies must
check in. Thank you for your cooperation.

Japanese Investments

Japanese investments circle this world today
and may capture the world tomorrow.

News Flash

News Flash: the UN passed a law, beginning in the year
2000 all calendars must be metric.

Mistakes

Attorneys get paid for mistakes and doctors bury theirs.

1948

Arizona and New Mexico Indians were permitted to vote.

Muggy

A muggy day is when everything that's suppose to stick together comes apart and everything that's suppose to come apart sticks together.

Peace

May the peace of God which passes all understanding, be with you now and always.

Allegiance

Remember: Politician's allegiance is only to politics.

Rights

We all got the right to be wrong.

Dieting Business

Dieting is a 30 billion a year industry.

Mistakes

Farmers and Ranchers take responsibility for their big expensive mistakes, but they often blame their foolish ones on their wives.

Past / Future

Do not regret the past and do not worry about the future.
Dhun-nun (Sufi)

Trust

Never trust one who cheats at playing solitaire.

Nevada

You can't beat the climate in Nevada,
you can't beat the slots either.

Life

The significance of life is life itself.
Herman Keyserling

Mistakes

Mistakes don't pay, the exception is alimony
where a woman makes money from her mistake.

Power

We have much power we have never used.

Learning

You can't learn anything any younger.

People

Nice people suck, mean people bite.

Clarity / Power

Write it down for clarity and power.

Arguing

Argue with a fool and become one.

Last Words

Just befor dieing Albert Einstein said something
to his nurse in German,
but she didn't speak or understand German.

Baseball
Baseball is ninety percent mental, the other half is physical.
Yogi Berra

Seattle
Day and nite cannot dwell together.
Seattle

Blinded
Blinded by hype & lies, most have been living in illusions
so long that the real world and truth are deeply buried.
Happy diggin

Symptoms
Symptoms are not the problem, but they point towards it.

Truth
How can you miss the water till the well runs dry?

Young / Old
Too young to be old, too old to be young.

Gettin There
Point yourself and take one step, then another, and another.

Great Plains
Overwhelming vastness,
buried in Buffalo gone to progress.

Statistics
Statistics are like bikinis;
What they reveal is interesting, what they conceal is vital.

Choices
Truth or Illusion, choose one, lose one

Sun Shines
The wise, the foolish, the sun shines equally on both.

Real Education
Real education & learning come from
studying that which we love.

Mocking Bird
I heard the mocking bird singing in the moonlight.
I knew, that moment, that I would get well.
Lone Wolf

Fear
Don't let fear steal your joy.

Humility
Humility is reminding self that we are no one
when others think we are somebody.

Nature
Nature does have manure and she does have roots
as well as blossoms, and you can't hate the
manure and blame the roots for not being blossoms.
R. Buckminster Fuller

1948
Arizona is forced by court decree to give
Indians the right to vote.

Humor

I realize humor isn't for everyone. It's only
for people who want to have fun, enjoy life, and feel alive.
Anne Wilson Schaef

Special

Any two ten dollar items for only $25.

Solitude

A wise man is never less alone than when he is alone.
Swift

Society

A man's interest in the world is
only the overflow of his interest in himself.
G.B. Shaw

Prayer

People would be surprised to know how much I learned
about prayer from playing poker.
Mary Austin

Pride

There is such a thing as a man being too proud to fight.
Woodrow Wilson

Healing

Most people get over illness in spite of the treatment.

Law

Screw the law, you get the guy off any way you can.
William Kunstler

Death & Life

Already made friends with death, still working on life.

Man's World

I don't mind living in a man's world
as long as I can be a woman in it.
Marilyn Monroe

Looked Over

It is better to be looked over than overlooked.
Mae West

Confusion

If you wander around in enough confusion,
you will soon find enlightenment.
Digby Diehl

Writing

Writing is a yoga that invokes your mind.
Allen Ginsberg

Avoid Trouble

To avoid trouble keep quiet and keep moving.

Dogmas

Dogmas always die of dogmatism.
Anais Nin

Fine Artist

A fine artist is one who makes familiar things
new and new things familiar.
Louis Nizer

Lookin & Talkin

Lookin & talkin about bulls ain't the same as ridin one.

Hours

What counts is not the number of hours you put in,
but how much you put in the hours.

Rest

Joy, temperance and repose
slam the door on the doctor's nose.

Fan

I'd much rather be having fun in the bedroom instead of
doing all this talking in the living room.
Elizabeth Ray

Maturing

You grow up by laughing at yourself.

People

Interesting people are people who are interested.
Bores are people who are bored.

Punishment

When the gods wish to punish us they answer our prayers.
Oscar Wilde

Happiness

Some cause happiness wherever they go,
others whenever they go.

Lonely

People are lonely because they
build walls instead of bridges.

Universal Language

Everywhere in the world people smile
in the same language.

Serenity

A serene man is able to enjoy the scenery on a detour.

Success

Try not to become a man of success but rather try
to become a man of value.
Albert Einstein

Change

Change yourself and everything changes.

Man / God

Which is it, is man one of God's blunders
or is God one of man's blunders?
Friedrich Wilhelm

Government

The incestuous relationship between government
and big business thrives in the dark.
Jack Anderson

Love

Love makes for good songs, stories & poems.

Faith

Faith goes out through the window when
beauty comes in at the door.
George Moore

Friends & Relatives

God gives us our relatives,
thank God we can choose our friends.
Ethel Mumford

Spouse

The plural of spouse is spice.
Christopher Morley

Pet Peeves

Pet peeves get petted too much.

Experience

One thorn of experience is worth a
whole wilderness of warning.
Lowell

Good Thing

Too much of a good thing can be wonderful.
Mae West

Children

Children are a great comfort in old age -
and they help you reach it faster too.

Eyes

It won't ruin your eyes to look at the bright side of things.

1950

Dillon Myer becomes commissioner of Indian Affairs
and a new program begins to move
Indians to cities and assimilation.

New

New day - New life.

Mind

Clutter your mind with little things and
there isn't room for big things.

The Best

The best is felt in the heart.

Opportunities

Opportunities look bigger going than coming.

Angels - Heaven

In heaven an angel is nobody in particular.
George Bernard Shaw

Life

Life is hard, by the yard but by the inch life's a cinch.

Fidelity

Absence makes the heart grow fonder, of somebody else.

Can't Be Done
He didn't know it couldn't be done and
went ahead and did it.

Ideas
The only ideas that will work for you
are the ones you put to work.

Discussion
Discussion is a sharing of knowledge,
argument is a sharing of ignorance.

Public Curiosity
The public have an insatiable curiosity to know everything
except what is worth knowing.
Oscar Wilde

Apples
Three apples make a glass of juice.

City / Wilderness
In the city you have civilization. In the wilderness we have
nature.

American Flag Tax Form
Printed in red, white and blue, when you've filled in the
white, you've left in the red and that makes you blue.

Succeed
The best way to succeed in life is to act on
the advice you give others.

Common Sense

An ounce of common sense is worth a pound of learning.

Be

Be brief, be bright, be gone.

Wisdom

What a fool does in the end,
a wise man does in the beginning.

Remember

When young remember you will be old,
when old remember you were young.

Seeing

We see things not as they are but as we are.

Talking

I'se alus mighty careful to stop and
taste mah words for I lets em pass mah teeth!

Right Or Wrong

Are you sure that you are right? How fine and strong,
but were you ever just as sure and wrong?

Flattery

Flattery is something nice someone tells
you about yourself that you wish was true.

Action / Habit

Every action contains the seed of a new habit.

Understanding
It is better to understand a little than to misunderstand a lot.

Responses
Do you act or react?

Good Manners
The sign of good manners is
putting up pleasantly with bad manners.

Money
Some people think they are worth
a lot of money because they have it.

Belief
Most hang on to their belief of what is right
no matter what the facts show.

Love
Love makes the world go round, and it can make you dizzy.

Return
You gave me love, I return joy, not in payment,
but to deepen our friendship.

Be Forgiving
Be forgiving of yourself and others.

1953
Termination Resolution calls for the end of federal protection while empowering states to take over civil and criminal
jurisdiction of Indian reservations without tribal consent.

Peaches

Ancient China, offerings of peaches to Gods,
ancestors and living elders for longevity.

Laughter

We don't laugh because we're happy,
we're happy because we laugh.

Hesitation

He who hesitates is last.
Mae West

Desire

Desire is the beginning of regret.

Spring In Nebraska

Ah - for the smell of spring in Nebraska,
the sweet aroma of wild plum blossoms.

Gifts

A man's gift makes room for him.

Saints and Deans

It is better to speak wisdom foolishly like the saints
than to speak folly wisely like the Deans.
Gilbert Chesteston

Knowledge

Everything I know I learned after I was thirty.
George Chemencean

Rules

Study the rules so you can properly break them.

Genius

Genius is one percent inspiration and
ninety-nine percent perspiration.
Thomas Edison

Flowers

Flowers have the most charm.

Endless Warfare

Chang-tzu said the horns of a snail were two
countries named man and chu that are engaged
in an endless cycle of warfare over the
empty space that stretched between them.

Lawyers

The first thing we do, let's kill all the lawyers.
Shakespeare

Civilized Men Arrived

Civilized men arrived in the pacific armed
with alcohol, syphilis, trousers and the bible.
Havelock Ellis

Pitching

Good pitching will always stop good hitting, and vice versa.
Casey Stengel

Anger

Cutting thru the anger, I found the core of love.

Elvis Prestley

Elvis didn't make his high school glee club.
Reason - couldn't sing well enough.

Confucius

Confusius attributes kindness to lovers of
mountains and wisdom to lovers of water.

Goodness

Be good and you will be lonesome.
Mark Twain

Epitaphs

The last quality in an epitaph is truth.
Henry David Thoreau

Money Versus Counsel

No man will take the counsel, but every man will take
money; therefore, money is better than counsel.
Jonathon Swift

Distinguishing Humans

What most distinguishes us humans
from lower animals is our desire to take drugs.
Lily Tomlin

Lies

People need good lies. There are too many bad one.
Kurt Vonnegut, Jr.

False American Myth
Teddy Roosevelt led the Rough Riders on their charge up Cubas San Juan Hill in the Spanish - American War. Reality is the unit was on foot and Roosevelt wasn't on San Juan Hill.

Verbal Contracts
A verbal contract isn't worth the paper it's written on.
Samuel Goldwyn

Suckers
Never give a sucker an ever break.
W.C. Fields

Wisdom
A wise man knows everything; a shrewd one, everybody.

Virtue
Many wish not so much to be virtuous, as to seem to be.
Cicero

Fads
Fads are painfully humorous, make or lose money and lack redeeming social value.

Shakespeare's Death
Assuming Francis Bacon was Shakespeare, he died as a result of stuffing snow into a chicken.

Jim Fixx
Jim Fixx the guru of jogging, the author of "The Complete Book of Running" died from a heart attack while jogging.

Judges

A judge is an attorney who's stopped practicing law.

Questions And Answers

Youth knows all the questions by
eight and all the answers by eighteen.

Having Children

Having children is a fetal mistake.

Filmmaking

Filmmaking is the process of turning money into light
and then back into money again.
John Boorman, Director

Wisdom

Transforming knowledge into wisdom is the ability to see
truths and recognize them for what they really are.
Fawn Journeyhawk Bender

Enlightened

Enlightenment means no longer able
to waste life chasing money.

Doctors

Lots of poor doctors but few doctors that are poor.

Supervisors

Supervisors delegate authority, shift blame
and take all the credit.

Rednecks

Rednecks eat with their fingers and talk with their forks.

Donald Duck

Donald Duck comics were banned in Finland
because he doesn't wear pants.

Parasites

Parasites live in Paris.

President Grover Cleveland

Cleveland is the only president to have previously
put the hoods on, tightened the nooses and sprung
the trap doors in a hanging.

Most Expensive Vehicle

The most expensive vehicle per mile is the shopping cart.

Price Of Freedom

In America freedom is worth any price,
and if you ain't got the money, you can't have it.

Ignorance Is Bliss

If ignorance is bliss, why aren't more people happy.

Schools

The schools ain't what they used to be and never was.
Will Rogers

1953

Maine Indians were allowed to vote.

Takin It With You

With the high cost of funerals today,
there's nothin left to take with you.

Skinning

Humans are the only animal that can
be skinned more than once.

Gigolos

Gigolos have what it takes to take what they have.

Success

A man owes success to his first wife
and his second wife to success.

Deserving

Those complaining about not getting
what they deserve, should be grateful.

No Match

Men are no match for women.

Tenses

The difference between tense and past tense is divorce.

Fame

What's fame, after all, me la-ad? it's as apt to be what
some man writes on ye'er tombstone.
E.P. Dunne

Temptation / Opportunity

Opportunity knocks but once, lightly,
temptations bangs loudly and continuously.

Mental Institution

A mental institution is either an insane asylum or a college.

Nudist

Ain't nothing wrong with being a nudist,
we're all born that way.

Inventors

An optimist invented the boat.
A pessimist invented the life preserver.

Doctor

A doctor is a person who enjoys bad health.

Falling

One falls in the direction one leans.

Height

The maximum distance between fingertips
with outstretched arms is your height.

Costs

Divorce costs more than weddings and is worth it.

Friends

Friends come and go and in the end you
need six to carry your coffin.

Honesty

There's one way to find out if a man's honest - ask him.
If he says yes, you know he is a crook.
Groucho Marx

Sugar Sweet?

Lemons contain more sugar than strawberries.

Death Then Life

In 1936 a jockey named Ralph Neves was pronounced
dead after a horse threw him then fell on him. The doctors
reported no heartbeat or pulse, he was hauled away by
ambulance. Neves awoke in cold storage, grabbed a
sheet, caught a cab back to the racetrack. He later won
the season's award for the jockey riding the most winers.

First Self Made Millionaire In A Communist Country

Erno Rubik the inventor of Rubik's Cube.

Dogma

You can't teach an old dogma new tricks.
Dorothy Parker

Jugular Vein

The jugular vein is an artery.

1953

American Indians allowed to buy alcohol
off reservations but not on reservations.

Advertising
Magazines and newspapers require about
fifty percent ads to survive.

Absorbed People
People today are absorbed in the material world created by
people, forgetting the natural world created by God.

Heavy Metal Termites
Under the influence of Heavy Metal Music
termites devour wood twice as fast.

TV Verses Sleeping
TV requires less calories than sleeping.

Rats
Rats can live longer without water than camels.

Eyes
The eyes of the dead are closed gently;
we also have to open gently the eyes of the living.
Jean Cocteau

Money
The average US man has $27 in his wallet.

Leading Troops
The emperor sent his troops to the field with immerse
enthusiasm, he will lead them in person, when they return.
Mark Twain

Ostriches

Ostriches do not bury their heads in sand.

Taverns

Taverns are places where madness is sold by the bottle.
Jonathon Swift

Riches

A man is rich in proportion to the number
of things which he can afford to leave alone.
Henry David Thoreau

Hair Brushes

Camel hair brushes are made from squirrel hair.

Holocausts

100,000 times worse than
the Jewish holocaust of Germany;
the Native America Holocaust of America.

Buffalo

There were more buffalo than there are cattle today.

Women

The greatest under-developed
natural resource in the world today.
Edward Steichen

Hair

Blondes have the most hair.

1961
US commission on Civil Rights reports
injustices in living conditions of Indians.

Brains
Brains are an asset - if you hide them.
Mae West

World Lesson
A world lesson is an experience.
It does not require translation into symbols or words
for you to remember it. It becomes part of what you know.
A word lesson seldom has this impact.
Harry Palmer

Intelligence Costs
The US government spends
100 million a day on intelligence.

Beauty
Always keep something beautiful in sight.

Col. Sanders
Kentucky Fried Chicken originator was born in Indiana.

Wisdom
Lor, Chile, when yuh ain't got no education,
yuh jes got to use yo brains.

Expensive Wedding Guest
$375 to bring Goofy to your Disney World wedding.

History

The best history is written by those who lived it.

Grounds For Divorce

A Delaware woman filed for divorce because
her husband regularly put itching powder
in her underwear when she wasn't looking.

Harry S. Truman

Never kick a fresh turd on a hot day.

Good ?

There is no man so good, who, were he to submit all
thoughts and actions to the laws, would not deserve
hanging ten times in his life.
Montaigne

Hanging

The thief is sorry he is to be hanged, not that he is a thief.

Scalping

Another European cruelty brought to America and
used on the Indians. When the Indians retaliated
in same they were discredited further by being
blamed as the source of scalping.

Bicyclists

Bicyclists have one serious accident every 10,000 miles.

Home

A hundred men can make an encampment,
but it requires a woman to make a home.

Haste

Haste makes waste.

Fathers

Children can find other children to be pals.
Children need fathers to be fathers.
Garrison Keillor

Single Girls Tips

Never look for a husband - look for a single man.

Hate

I do desire we may be better strangers.
Shakespeare

Sing Enthusiastically

Sing Enthusiastically the song of life.

Genius

It is with rivers as it is with people; the greatest are
not always the most agreeable nor the best to live with.
Henry Van Dyke

God

I believe in the incomprehensibility of God.

Hardship

Misfortune and pain lead to much truth.

Fools

No one is a fool always, every one sometimes.

Women Are A Problem

Women are a problem, but if you haven't already guessed, they're the kind of problem I enjoy wrestling with.
Warren Beatty

Scarce

Scarce as upper teeth in a cow.

Religion

Religion is what keeps the poor from murdering the rich.
Napoleon Bauaparte

Fortune

Fortune does not change men; it unmasks them.
Mane Necker

Friendship

Friendship is love without it's wings.
Byron

Clothing

Better go to heaven in rags than to hell in embroidery.

1962

New Mexico forced by federal government
to give Indians voting rights.

Common Complaint

The complaint of these times is the complaint of all times.

Aging

I'm old enough to know my future is shorter than my past.

Smiling

Start every day with a smile, and get it over with.
W.C. Fields

Conscience

Conscience is mostly projection of other opinions.

Contentment

Enjoying what you have without desiring more.

Dinner

Dinner was made for eatin not for talkin.
Thackeray

Wisdom And Advice

We admire the wisdom of those who seek our advice.

Laughter

Only fools don't laugh.

Men

A man not handsome at twenty,
not strong at thirty, not rich at forty, not wise at fifty,
will never be handsome, strong, rich or wise.

Life

Life is like a ladder. Every step we take
is either up or down.

Growth

You've got to do your own growing
on matter how tall your grandfather was.

Man Of Action

A man of action, forced into a state of thought,
is unhappy until he can get out of it.
Galsworthy

Painting / Poetry

Painting is silent poetry,
and poetry is painting with the gift of speech.
Simonides

Christians

Scratch the Christian and you find the pagan - spoiled.
Israel Zangwill

Doing / Not Doing

Doing is life, not doing is death.

Temptation

The only way to get rid of a temptation is to yield to it.
Oscar Wilde

Spelling

I don't give a damn for a man that
can spell a word only one way.
Mark Twain

Vacations

Vacations are taking a rest from work to
return to work more in need of rest than before.

Money Economy

Everyone sells something to get money to survive.

Credit

Soldiers win battles and generals get the credit.
Napoleon

Wealth

God shows his contempt for wealth
by the kind of person he selects to receive it.
Austin O'Malley

Temptation

I generally avoid temptation - unless I can't resist it.
Mae West

Women

Any women in the world, even a nun,
would rather lose her virtue than her reputation.
Lionel Stachey

Birth Control

My views on birth control are somewhat distorted by
the fact that I was seventh of nine children.
Robert F. Kennedy

Promises

Promises and piecrust are made to be broken.
Jonathan Swift

Youth

Youth is a wonderful thing.
What a crime to waste it on children.
George Bernard Shaw

Poor Progress

A new Wal-Mart opens every two days.

Save Your Breath

People won't take warnings or advice.

1964

Conference on Indian poverty is held in Washington, D.C.

Hell

Hell is a city very much like London.
Percy Shelley

Flowers

Isn't it odd that flowers are the reproductive
organs of the plants they grow on.
Logan Smith

Before And After Marriage

Before marriage, a man will lie awake
all night thinking about something you said;
after marriage, he'll fall asleep before you finish saying it.
Helen Rowland

TV Concerns

Why are people more concerned about sex than violence?

Historian

The historian is a prophet looking backwards.
Angust Schlegel

Big Business Investment
Big business advice: Invest in America—Buy Congressman.

Bombs
Kick the bomb habit.

Beneficial Gay Marriages
One of the benefits of gay marriages is that irresponsible
sex doesn't add to the population problem.

Gun Runners
The United States is the number one
arms merchant of the world.

Hypocrisy
Larry Flint is cussed for exposing hypocrisy when
the respectable sanctioned media doesn't.

White Collar Crime
White collar crime generally receives little punishment,
none when involves government.

Gigolo
A gigolo is a fee-male.
Isaac Goldberg

Women To Women Advice
"Men can't be fixed"

Cats
Cats are made uneasy by rocking chairs.

We Need More Bargains

We need more B-1 bombers at the bargain price
of only $500 million each.

Relationship Problems

What can you expect other than relationship problems
from people who learned about relationships
from watching soap operas.

Dead Atheist

A dead atheist is someone who's
all dressed up with no place to go.

Living

Stop, look & listen.

War

There will be more wars until
men grow brave enough to stop them.

Wisdom

Wisdom comes by disillusionment.
Santayana

Giving

As a child I understood how to give; I have forgotten
this grace since I became civilized.
Ohiyesa

Duty

Duty is pretending that the unimportant is important.

Today
Keep one foot in yesterday and one foot in tomorrow
and shit all over today.

Twelve Steps
Your elevator is shut down, you'll just have to use the steps.

Doing
If you let other people do it for you, they will do it to you.
Robert Anthony

Old Dogs
There's nothing like an old dog with new tricks.

Self Pity
Self pity in its early stages is as snug as a feather mattress.
Only when it hardens does it become uncomfortable.
Maya Angelou

Equal Opportunities
Addictions are equal opportunity diseases.
Harvey Milkman

Punishment
One of the ways to punish those we love
is to withhold our feelings from them.

Berkley Students 1964
You can learn more from a jail than a university.

Love
Give and take a lot of love from a lot of people

Out

It is easier to stay out than to get out.
Mark Twain

Tongue

Tongue often hang man quicker than rope.
Charlie Chan

Marvelous Housekeeper

I am a marvelous housekeeper.
Every time I leave a man, I keep his house.
Zsa Zsa Gabor

Horses

Horses need shoes if hoof wear exceeds hoof growth.

New Philosophy

I have a new philosophy;
I'm only going to dread one day at a time.
Charles M. Schultz

Red Flags

Now when I see a red flag go up in a situation,
I know that it means caution. Before I started my recovery,
I thought it meant charge.
Anne Wilson Schaef

Tombstone Epitaph

To my wonderful husband John P. Smith.
May he rest in peace... until we meet again.

There Ain't A Cowman Alive

There ain't a cowman alive that can remember long ago
when you could borrow money, pay interest,
raise a family, raise cows & calves, sell the calves,
pay off your loans and save money too.

After You Know

After you know, you can't go back.

Rich

He was as rich as the full moon is shy.

Mirror Messages

Write on the top of your mirror
"this person is not to be taken seriously."

For Joy

For joy, don't read the newspapers, except for the comics.

Stress

When you can't stand any more stress go
to the washing machine and throw in the towel.

Government

The main problem with government is that they govern.

Unsuccessful Farm Wife

A unsuccessful farm wife was one whose chickens
got out and ate the garden then were eaten
by coyotes resulting in a hungry family.

The South

The South has a lot of Robert E. Lee High Schools.

Too Close

Hate & love, good & evil can be too close.

Special

Special one way dignitary flights from Washington DC to Oregon for legal doctor assisted suicides.

We Die

We die, become clouds, bring rain for new life.

Founding Fathers

Many of the founding fathers of USA were Deists.

Crime Poll

Crime poll reveals that 90% say there's too much legal crime while only 80% say there's too much illegal crime.

Love

He broke her heart and lost his.

SOB's

New Yorkers & Texans are SOB's, at least New Yorkers don't pretend to be somethings else.

Cheerful

She was as cheerful as Christmas cards.

He Was

He was too handsome for virtue & too young for wisdom.

Laps

I've been in more laps than a napkin.
Mae West

Church Bulletin

Don't let worry kill you, let the church help.

1964

Office of Economic Opportunity is created,
with an Indian desk sponsoring antipoverty programs.

Wisdom

Though a man be wise,
It is no shame for him to live and learn.
Sophocles

Cities

Cities cramp the soul.

Stood Up Wife

Note left for husband "Honey I went shopping -
your dinner is in the dog."

Cliches

Let's have some new cliches.
Samuel Goldwyn

Time

Time is just a state of mind.

Love

Those who are faithless know the pleasures of love;
it is the faithful who know love's tragedies.
Oscar Wilde

Change

Make one change at a time.

Mouth

A good time to keep your mouth shut is
when you're in deep water.

TV Advertising

Practicing medicine without a brain.

Leadership

Leadership is the ability to get men to do
what they don't want to do, and like it.
Harry Truman

Each Day

Each day life begins anew.

Lamaze

In Lamaze the partners role is to
remind the mother to be to breathe.

Bumper Sticker

Research and test humans, save animals.

Psychic

No matter what goes wrong,
there are those who knew it would.

Interchangeable Parts

Interchangeable parts aren't.

Meeting

The length of the meeting is the
square of the number present.

Paper

Paper is always strongest at the perforations.

Events

If something happens to you,
it has previously happened to your friends.

Coyote Sez

Coyote sez make chaos out of order.

Words

Words are the freezing of reality.
Timothy Leary

Find Yourself

In order to find yourself, you must lose yourself.

What Is Comedy

Comedy is the art of making people
laugh without making them puke.
Steve Martin

Situational Experience
It was a situation where it wasn't possible to have enough experience.

Moment
In a moment of peace & clarity,
I understood that I was drowning.

Humor
Humor exposes truth.

Computers
Computers require being treated as retarded
but obedient children.

Vultures Sitting & Waiting In A Tree
One vulture said to another
"patience my ass, let's go kill something."

Critters
Four legged critters are less confusin than two legged one.

Defiance, Resentment & Fear Defined
Defiance: I don't want to. Resentment: I shouldn't have to.
Fear: I can't.

Gentleman
A gentleman is one who never hurts
anyone's feeling unintentionally.
Oscar Wilde

The Code

They don't live by the code of the west out west anymore.

Men Like

Men like women who like to listen to them talk.

1964

U.S. Civil Rights Act prohibits discrimination for reasons of color, race, religion or national origin.

Cooling

Phoenix late 1920's - a cafe cut a large hole in the end wall and used a big fan to draw air thru a pad of wet horsehair, increasing business with one of the first commercial evaporative coolers.

Omaha, NE

The strategic air command chose Omaha for their headquarters because no one would care if it got bombed.

Super Salesman

Super salesman, super slick, could talk a doorknob into thinkin it was a dinner bell.

Tough

When the going gets tough, the tough, lighten up!
Terry Branerman

Birds of Prey

The female bird of prey is about 1/3 larger than the male.

Doctor Translations

I'd like to prescribe a new drug, translates to , I'm
writing a paper and would like to use you for a guinea pig.

On Marriage

Old cowboy said I've punched cows for low pay
all over the west for over forty years. Knowed some
might fine gals, but old time cowboyin weren't no kinda
life for a wife. Now when I see a happy couple, think
I missed somethin but when I see a poor old
hen pecked husband, think I escaped somethin.

Don't Tell

Don't tell those who can't listen.

Promises

He promised her the moon & she still has it to look at.

Misunderstood

People who are "misunderstood" generally
don't explain themselves enough.

Rainy Day

A rainy day ain't worth savin for.

Cowboy Grass

Some cowboys eat grass, some smoke it too.

Seals

Whatta mean I can't kill em?
Rod Miller Jr., Navy Seal

Highroller

A top hand only at puttin on the dog.

Women & Cats

Men can never figure out either.

Your God Is Too Small

Expand your God to include the Gods
of all religions & beliefs.

110° Heat

People living in Phoenix Arizona sometimes
complain about the 110° summer heat. Easterners
tell 'em it's easier to shovel 110° than three feet of snow.

Work

He was absorbed in work like crackers in soup.

Watch

Watch the moon rise. Watch the moon set.
Watch the sun rise. Watch the sun set.

Celebrate

Join bodies and celebrate the center.

Clever

The cleverest thing you could do
would be to give up your cleverness.

Life's choices
Loving, and not loving.

Women Are Like Phones
Love to be talked to, love to be held,
but if you push the wrong button, you're disconnected.

Keep Working
Keep working, millions on welfare are depending on you.

Guns
1998 Gun laws: In Australia it became illegal for citizens
to own guns. A brigade of USA Marines
assisted in removing private guns.

Passion
Passion eventually changes to pension.

Art
We all know that art is not truth.
Art is a lie that makes us realize truth.
Pablo Picasso

Do You Pray For The Senators?
No. I look at the senators and pray for the country.
Edward Everett Hale, Senate Chaplain 1903-1909

Colorado River
The Colorado River: too thick to swim, too thin to plow.

Evolution

Arizona stick lizards are ordinary lizards who have evolved to carrying sticks in their mouths during the hot summer desert days. During the hottest part of the afternoon, the lizard lays his stick on the ground and climbs up on it, getting relief from the hot sand. Recent observations reveal a small percentage of stick lizards have started to jab their sticks in the ground and then climb up the stick for even more relief from the heat.

People

The trouble with most people is their trouble.

Names

Plumber & Leek, plumbing firm in Norfolk, England.

War Movies

War movies don't show what war is really like, therefore, there has never been a good war movie.

Gift

Your gift to the world is your radiance.

Mystery

There is mystery in everything.

Life

Life is ending.

Lent

I gave up sanity for lent.

Knowing

Knowing comes when it comes.

Mating

Ten percent of the males do ninety percent of the mating.

1965

Voting Rights Act ensures equal voting rights.

Rain & Ants

Ants travel in a straight line before rain,
scatter for fair weather.

Keeping Warm

Wearing a hat keeps your feet warm.

Medical Students

Older medical students are more likely to
become general practitioners.

Inspections

Look at the underneath part.

Eclipses

Sun & moon eclipses often happen
in pairs with a 2 week space between them.

Fate

Destiny leads the willing,and drags the unwilling.

Dehydrated Water

Arizona ranchers are raising cattle on dehydrated water, among the many advantages is eliminating the high cost of beef processing. These ranchers are making a lot of money in a low income industry by slicing up their beef and selling it directly to consumers as beef jerky.

Heaven

Whenever cannibals are on the brink of starvation, Heaven in its infinite mercy sends them a nice plump missionary.
Oscar Wilde

The Future

I never think of the future. It comes soon enough.
Albert Einstein

Microwave

You can microwave in a metal container minimum ratio of 2/3 food to 1/3 metal.

Blackjack

The dealer will usually go broke with an upcard of 5.

Making Friends

You can make more friends in two months by becoming interested in other people than you can in two years by trying to get people interested in you.
Dale Carnegie

Last Words

Two Gun Crowley, strapped to the electric chair said "you sons of bitches. Give my love to mother."

Consciousness History

Only rarely in all the history of consciousness have there existed individuals capable of guiding beings through the labyrinth of creation back to life source.

Millions there have been who have worn the garments of priests and holy men, but in ignorance or worse have only managed to divert beings into elaborately constructed belief systems for elaborately constructed reasons—blind alleys of sorrow far from home.
Harry Palmer

Equipment

Buy a new piece of equipment only if it will pay for itself in three months.

Water

Drink water often enough & quantity enough that you are never thirsty.

Teenager

A teenager is most likely to leave home at age 18.

Hospital

Avoid going to the hospital in July as thats when all the new interns start.

Exercise

One hour of being physically active lengthens your life 2 hours.

Opportunity
Never refuse a good offer.

Church Bulletin
Weight Watchers will meet at 7 p.m. Thursdays,
please use large double door on the south side.

Optimism
The place where a optimism most flourishes
is the lunatic asylum.
Havelock Ellis

Gay President
Our 15th president James Buchanan was gay.

Knot
A knot reduces the strength of a rope 50%.

Car Theft
Two door cars are stolen twice as often as four doors.

Sunset
The sun disappears in 2 minutes
after it touches the horizon.

Love And Marriage
I loved her far too much to marry.

Yuma
In the 1800's a soldier died in Yuma Arizona
and of course went to hell. He requested blankets
because he was chilly.

Aging

You are old when your wedding presents
are sold as antiques.

Clothes

Horizontal lines make you look fat,
vertical lines make you look taller & thinner.

Clothing Sizes

Sizes in clothing tend to run smaller outside the USA.

Cowboy Hat

It takes 2-6 hours to make a cowboy hat.

Run Don't Walk

Run don't walk on the slippery, fragile,
razors edge between safety & crazy fun.

More Rain

Drops of rain hanging on a wire clothesline
mean another rain soon.

Moon

The moon rises 50 minutes later each day.

Duck Hunting

When the wind is in the east, ducks fly the least.
Ed Timmerman

Milk

A cow drinks 3# of water to make 1# of milk.

Predicting Storms
Children and other younger animals
get wilder before a storm.

Child Advice
Never fill a childs glass over half full.

Luck & Skill
Luck is when you win. Skill is when I win.

Adversity
Adversity finds at last the man whom
she has often passed by.
Seneca

Fingernails
Fingernails grow faster on long fingers.

General Sherman
On Indians. Extermination is the only answer. The more
we kill this year, the less we will have to kill next year.

Dairy Cow
A dairy cow eats 6 tons of alfalfa per year.

Storms
Red sunrise, a ring around the moon,
smoke laying down all indicate a storm coming.

Do
Do good things anonymously.

Cruise

On a cruise to help prevent seasickness
get a cabin near the ships center of gravity.

Don't

Don't gamble.

Selling

The best months to sell by mail are September,
January and November.

Love

Love passes quickly, and passes like a street Arab,
anxious to mark his way with mischief.
Balzac

Teakettle Forecast

Teakettles sing before a storm.

Naps

A mid day nap of 1/2 to one hour equals
2 to 3 hours sleep at nite.

1968

American Indian Civil Right Act extends Bill of Right
protection to reservation Indians. It bars states from
assuming law and order jurisdictions on reservations
without tribal consent. It applies same restrictions to
tribal governments as to federal and state governments.

Early Cooling
The first mechanically cooled Hotel lobby was in Phoenix Arizona at the Hotel Adams where electric fans blew over pans of ice.

Successful Landing
A successful landing is any landing you walk away from.

Corn
2000# corn make 50 gallons of ethanol.

Deer Forecast
When you see deer feeding in the early afternoon, expect a change in weather.

Laws & Corruption
More laws, more corruption.

Two Kinds Of Women
There are only two kinds of women - goddesses and doormats.
Pablo Picasso

Driving
Ten percent of late nite drivers are under the influence.

News
And that's the way it is -- and most of the time we hope it isn't.
Walter Cronkite

Money And Women
A woman expects you to spend $3 to her $1.

Nixon

If they want to put me in jail, let them.
The best writing by politicians has been done in jail.
Richard Nixon

Expectations

Don't expect anything better than
institutional food from institutions.

Awareness

Probably the biggest bring down in my life
was being in a pop group and finding out just how
much it was like everything it was supposed to be against.
Mama Cass Elliot

Oranges

A cup of juice from two oranges.

Failure

There is the greatest practical benefit in
making a few failures early in life.
T.H. Huxley

Cantaloupe Ripeness

A cantaloupe is ripe when it has a musky smell.

Drugs

The best mind altering drug is truth.
Lily Tomlin

1968

American Indian movement (AIM) is founded.

Sleeping Progress

It has gone from feeling guilty for sleeping with someone
to feeling guilty if you're not sleeping with someone.

Time

Time wounds all heels.
Ann Landers

Trends

I don't set trends, I just find out
what they are and I exploit them.
Dick Clark

Desert Refrigerator

Early Arizona desert refrigerators consisted of
a wood frame covered with burlap, a can of water
with pinholes allowing water to seep onto the burlap.
As the water evaporated from the burlap,
it cooled the apparatus and contents.

Facts

No facts to me are sacred, none are profane.
Emerson

Sailing

Wind before rain; you'll be sailing again.
Rain before wind; take your sails in.

Prayer

O ye Gods, grant us what is good whether we pray for it or
not, but keep evil from us even though we pray for it.
Plato

Big Time

On stage I make love to twenty-five thousand people,
then I go home alone.
Janis Joplin

Perception

Everyone else is talking about how hard life is,
and here I am singing about how good it is to be alive.
John Denver

Evolution

Evolution has her own accounting system
and that's the only one that matters.
R. Buckininster Fuller

Henry Miller

To enter life by way of the vagina is as good a way as any.

Mother Of The Year

The mother of the year should be a sterilized
woman with two adopted children.
Paul Ehrlick

Casinos

Stay in a casino long enough and they throw you out.

1969

N. Scott Momaday, a Kiowa, is awarded the pulitzer
prize for his novel "The House Made Of Dawn".

Threatening

Most people do not want to understand nature.

Progress

Progress might have been all right once,
but it's gone on too long.
Ogden Nash

Delta Fuel

Delta Airlines uses 7.5 million gallons of fuel per day.

Respect Plumbers & Philosophers

We must have respect for both our plumbers
and our philosophers or neither our pipes
or our theories will hold water.
John W. Gardner

Your Stride

Your leg length equals your walking stride.

Payment

It has to pay good in money
and/or satisfaction before anyone will do it.

Intelligence

Man is unique among animals in his
practiced ability to know things that are not so.
Philip Slater

White Race

The white race is the cancer of history.
Susan Sontag

Truth

Truth is illusion burned up.

Easier

People can dream, cry & laugh much
easier than they can change.

Experience

Experience is not what happens to a man.
It is what a man does with what happens to him.
Aldous Huxley

Life

There is more to life than increasing its speed.
Mahatma Gandhi

Movements

All movements go too far.
Bertrand Russell

You Gotta Go

You gotta go thru hell to get to heaven.

Religious

I do benefits of all religious: I'd hate to blow
the here after on a technicality.
Bob Hope

Ambition

Ambition is never satisfied.

Suffering

Although the world is very full of suffering,
it is also full of the overcoming of it.
Helen Keller

Advice
Don't rain on other people's parades.

Progress
Textile manufactures in the eastern United States used moisture to clean the air in their mills and discovered they had invented the evaporative cooler.

Three Sins
There are only three sins - Causing pain, causing fear, causing anguish. The rest is window dressing.
Roger Caras

Time
There is more time than life.

Codependent Light Bulb
How many codependents does it take to change a light bulb? Twelve! One puts in the bulb and the other eleven give directions and advice.

Pleasure / Pain
In pleasure or in pain, give neither free rein.

Money
God provides lots of money to the affluent because they couldn't survive without it.

President Ronald Reagan
We made no progress at all.. and we didn't intend to. That's the function of the national committee.
Ronald Reagan

Truth
Truth suffers but never perishes.

Humble
Don't be humble, you're not that great.
Golda Meir

Waco Guilt
Guilty without a doubt. Politically incorrect beliefs.

Nite
God created nite as a gift for the sinners.

Politics
I don't think politics is a workable system any more..
They gotta invent something better.
David Crosby

Mailorders
In selling by mail 2 orders per 100 mail outs is excellent.

Trust
Trust your friend the same as your enemy.

1969 - 71
Indian occupation of Alcatraz Island.

Fine Schools
Many have gone to fine schools for
years only to become fools.

Will

Where there's a will there's a way.

New Beginnings

When you live in the present,
every moment is a new beginning.

Today

Don't do today what you can delay until manana.

Unitarians

Unitarians bring their own God to church.

Age

The old believe everything, the middle-aged suspect
everything, the young know everything.
Oscar Wilde

The Dead

The dead stay in the ground, while the living fool around.

Run With Wolves

Run with wolves and learn to howl.

Youth / Age

With youth, it's dreams; with age, it's memories.

Common Sense And Good Taste

He's a man of great common sense and good taste, meaning thereby a man without originality or moral courage.
George Bernard Shaw

Doctor Translations

This should be taken care of right away, translates to: I've planned an expensive trip and I need the money right away.

Hope

He who lives with hope dies happy.

Women

After thirty-five a man begins to have thoughts about women; before that age he has feeling.
Austin O'Malley

Timely

Better one timely squawk, than constant talk.

Fort Cobb Address

You cut down our trees. You slaughter our Antelope and the Buffalo, and yet you do not eat, but leave them to rot. You dig into Mother Earth and toss your waste in our streams that one time were clear.
You burn everything. What do you want? Are you crazy?
Satanta (Kiowa)

Means

Live below your means.

Funny

Everything is funny, as long as it is happening to somebody else.
Will Rogers

Class
Teach a class. Be a student in a class.

Life
Life is easier to take than you'd think;
all that is necessary is to accept the impossible,
do without the indispensable, and bear the intolerable.
Kathleen Norris

Responsibility
Take responsibility for all parts of your life.

Toilet Seats
How many men does it take to put the toilet seat down?
Nobody knows, it hasn't happened yet.

Mistakes
Admit your mistakes and make amends.

Better Person
May you always be the kind of person
your dog thinks you are.

Sperm
Why does it take 1 million sperm to fertilize 1 egg?
They won't ask for directions.

Do
Take Walks.

Aging

The only time we desire to be older
is when we are children.

Apache Peace

That this race are destined to a speedy and final extinction,
seems to admit of no doubt... all that can be expected
from an enlightened and Christian government, such as
ours, is to graduate and smooth the passing of their
final exit from the state of human existence.
E.A. Graves, Indian Bureau Agent, Washington on Apaches
during the peace before the Apache wars.

Others

Amuse, but don't abuse.

Sex

Why do men become smarter during sex with a women?
Because they are plugged into a genius.

Womens Problems

The problem with most women is they get
all excited about nothing, then they marry him.

Bears

Bears can outrun, out climb and out swim humans
except in running downhill.

Shermans Apostle

On Indians. The only good Indian is a dead Indian.
Sheridan

Suspended

Suspended in spiritual ecstasy.

Life

May you live all the days of your life.
Swift

Church Air

One should not go in churches if one
wants to breath pure air.
Friedrich Wilhelm

Willa Cather

The Willa Cather Pioneer Memorial denies that
Nebraska's most enduring writer was a lesbian.

Evangelist Spells

Evangelist = Evil's agent

Bounties

Central City, Colorado $25. Deadwood City,
South Dakota $200. Massachusetts $400.
Many "respectable" citizens made a good living
as Indian killers collecting the scalps bounties.

Seekers Advice

My advice to knowledge seekers has always been
"evaluate" not "judge", "challenge" not "attack",
"show me" not "prove it".
Fawn Journeyhawk Bender

Cheating Suicides

Before Kovorkian suicides cheated doctors out of work.

Nice Guy

More or less a nice guy, more some days, less some days.

Easy

Black and white are easy.
The hard part is that 85% of life is grey.

Arizona Heat

Arizona has a dry heat in summer which usually feels cool.
In the summer of 1990 temperatures hit 122 and all agreed
that Arizona heat was hot heat!

You

His majesty, the body, that brat is self,
wants what it wants - NOW!

1970

Blue lake taken in 1906 is
returned to Taos Pueblo in land swap.

Jewelry

Over a hundred Americans a day get injured by jewelry.

Marijuana

Queen Victoria of England smoked
marijuana to cure her cramps.

The National Anthem
Believe It Or Not

In 1920 Ripley reported that the US didn't have an official national anthem. Over five million Americans signed petitions requesting Congress to designate one. In 1931 "The Star-Spangled Banner" become the official national anthem.

Lingerie Study

75% of women wear the wrong size bra.

Television

I must say I find television very educational.
The minute somebody turns it on
I go int the library and read a good book.
Groucho Marx

Funerals

A third of Taiwanese funerals include a stripper.

Helping

If you pick up a starving dog and make him prosperous, he will not bite you; that is the principal difference between a dog and a man.
Mark Twain

Constipation

Constipation causes the most death in fruit flies.

Coney Island

Coney Island: where the surf is
one third water and two thirds people.
John Steinbeck

NY Cab Drivers

90% are recent immigrants.

First Animated TV Ad

The first animated TV ad was created for
Ford Motor Co. in 1949 by Dr. Seuss.

Presidential Winner

Mr. Rogers is the preschool presidential choice.

November 19th

November 19th is Have a Bad Day Day.

Plumbing

First American with indoor
plumbing was Longfellow in 1840.

Reno Directions

From Los Angeles go north a lot and a little west.

Rich And Poor

I've been rich, and I've been poor,
and believe me, rich is better.
Joe E. Lewis

Men's Clothing

Two thirds of men's clothing is purchased by women.

Early

Early to bed, early to rise,
and your girl goes out with other guys.
Bob Collins

Football Cows

The National Football League uses
3000 cowhides a year for footballs.

Early Contraceptive

2000 BC, crocodile dung used by Egyptians.

Eyes

Starfish have an eye at the end of each of their eight legs.

Genghis Khan

His army rode mares for the benefit of fresh milk.

Amherst College

Amherst College in Massachusetts is named after Jeffrey
Amherst, who first initiated germ warfare in the Americas
(smallpox infected blankets given to the Indians).

War

A great war leaves the county with three armies - an army of
cripples, an army of mourners, and an army of thieves.

Gorillas

Gorillas stick out their tongues when angry.

Church Bulletin

Remember in prayer the many who
are sick of our church and community.

Daylight Savings Time

Accidents increase 10% the first week of the time change.

Toughest Fake

Palisades Nevada fooled the world with fake gunfights for three years earning the title "the toughest town in the west".

Wisdom & Education

Wisdom is ever a blessing;
education is sometimes a curse.
John Shedd

Taste

I would rather be able to appreciate things I can not have
than to have things I am not able to appreciate.
Elbert Hubbard

Temptation

The woman tempted me, and tempts me still!
Lord God, I pray you that she ever will!
E.V. Cooke

False American Myth

Charles Lindbergh was the first person to fly nonstop across the Atlantic. Reality, He was the 67th person, the first was William Alcock and Arthur Brown in 1919, eight years earlier. Lindbergh was the first to do it alone.

Pet Owners

The real problem with pet owners is that the pets are
smarter that they are.

Thought

There is nothing either good or bad,
but thinking makes it so.
Shakespeare

1972

Trail of Broken Treaties Caravan. AIM occupies offices of
BIA in Washington, D.C.

Time

The years teach much which the days never know.
Emerson

Money / Acting

I went into the business for the money, and the art
grew out of it. If people are disillusioned by
the remark, I can't help it. Its the truth.
Charlie Chaplin

Reality

Reality is something you rise above.
Liza Minnelli

Suspenders

Mark Twain was issued a patent for suspenders in 1871.

Aging

Everyone wants to live a long time, no one wants to be old.

Truth

Truth uttered before its time is always dangerous.
Mencius

Understanding

There are three things I have always loved and never
understood, painting, music, women.
Fontenelle

Sacrifice
In this world it is not what we take up,
but what we give up that makes us rich.
H.W. Beecher

Smell
I would rather smell of nothing than of perfume.
Martial

First Love
First love is only a little foolishness and a lot of curiosity.
George Bernard Shaw

Jokes
I don't make jokes, I just watch the government
and report the facts.
Will Rogers

Solitude
I never found the companion that was
so companionable as solitude.
Thoreau

Pretending
We become what we pretend to be.
Kurt Vonnegut, Jr.

Cats
Calico cats are female.

Speeches
Do not say all that you know,
but always know what you say.
Claudian

Prejudice
I am free of all prejudices. I hate everyone equally.
W.C. Fields

Indian Meaning Of Mount Rushmore
Mt. Rushmore's big white faces and telling that first
we gave you Indians a treaty that you could keep
these Black Hills forever . . . in exchange for all the
Dakotas, Wyoming and Montana. Then we found gold
and took this piece of land, because we were stronger . . .
And after we did all this, we carved up this mountain,
the dwelling place of your spirits, and put our four
gleaming white faces here. We are the conquerors.
Lame Deer, Dakota Leader

Stupidity
There is no sin except stupidity.
Oscar Wilde

Price
Everything is worth what the purchaser will pay for it.
Publilins Syrus

Preachers
Clergyman: I've lost my briefcase. Traveller:
I pity your grief. Clergyman: My sermons are in it.
Traveller: I pity the thief.

Punishment

We are not punished for our sins, but by them.
Elbert Hubbard

Argument

The only way to get the best of an argument is to avoid it.
Dale Carnagie

Reason

The heart has reasons that reason does not understand.
Bossuet

Remorse

It is sweeter to be remorseful over past sins
than regretful about lost opportunities.

Philosophy

Philosophy did not find Plato a nobleman, it made him one.
Seneca

1972

White vigilantes beat Raymond Yellow Thunder to death in
Gordon, NE. Suicide ruling protested, officials forced to do
autopsy; two of the killers are tried and convicted.

Pity

There is no suffering which pity will not insult.

Romance

Romance has been elegantly defined
as the offspring of fiction and love.
Disraeli

Avatar

The mission of Avatar in the world is to catalyze the integration of belief systems.

When we perceive that the only difference between us is our beliefs and that beliefs can be created or discreated with ease, the right and wrong game will wind down, a co-create game will unfold, and world peace will ensue.
Harry Palmer

Cows / Rain

Cows don't graze before a rain.

Prejudices

Prejudice is the reason of fools.
Voltaire

Opportunity

A pessimist is one who makes difficulties of his opportunities; an optimist is one who makes opportunities of his difficulties.
Vice-Admiral Mansell, R.N.

The Past

I used to be Snow White - but I drifted.
Mae West

Broadway

Broadway is a place where people spend money they haven't earned to buy things they don't need to impress people they don't like.
Walter Winchell

Optimism

Keep your face to the sun and you cannot see the shadow.
Helen Keller

Passion

It is the weak who can control their passions,
they have such weak passions.

Originality

Originality is simply a pair of fresh eyes.
T.W. Higginson

Medicine

More die from the medicine than from the illness.

Perseverance

Diligence is the mother of good luck.
Franklin

Money

That for which all virtue now is sold
and almost every vice, almighty gold.
Ben Jonson

Moral Choice

Indulge or preach.

Lady

A lady is one who never shows
her underwear unintentionally.
Lillian Day

73 Tavern Sign
No time is wasted when you're wasted in Herman, Nebraska

Womans Rights
Every woman has the right to be immoral if she wants to be.

Music
Music is the universal language of mankind.
Longfellow

Population
The world added more people between 1950 and 2000
"than in the four million years since humans stood upright."
Lester Brown, Environmentalist

Nature
Nature is the art of God.

Marriage
Men do not know their wives well;
but wives know their husbands perfectly.
Feuillet

Noise
People who make no noise are dangerous.

Fear
Unresolved fear eventually results in illness.
Fawn Journeyhawk Bender

White Man's Burden
The white man's greatest burden is a lot of other white men.

Opportunity
The secret of success in life is for a man to
be ready for his opportunity when it comes.
Disraeli

Mercy
Being all fashioned of the self-same dust,
Let us be merciful as well as just.
Longfellow

Misanthrope
A misanthrope I can understand, a womanthrope never.
Oscar Wilde

Mistakes
Woman was God's "second" mistake.
Nietzche

Money
The use of money is all the advantage there is in having it.
Franklin

Happiness
A man can be happy with any woman as
long as he does not love her.
Oscar Wilde

Advice
Always act like you know what you're doing
and where you're going.

Movie Music

This music won't do, there's not enough sarcasm in it.
Samuel Goldwyn

Perfect Wife

The perfect wife is a big corn fed NE woman.
She'll provide shade in the summer & warmth in the winter.

Luck

Luck is like the weather, it will change.

1973

AIM and 200 Lakota occupy site of Wounded Knee
Massacre at Pine Ridge. Two Indians killed.

Man

God made man a little lower than the angels, and he has
been getting a little lower ever since.
Will Rogers

Logic

Logic: an instrument used for bolstering a prejudice.
Elbert Hubbard

C Students

The C students run the world.
Harry Truman

Wisdom

If I were wiser, I wouldn't be where I am now, but of course
if I weren't where I am now, how could I get any wiser?
Anne Wilson Schaef

Moon Love

Love is like the moon;
when it does not increase it decreases.
Segur

Education

The bookful blockhead, ignorantly read,
with loads of learned lumber in his head.
Pope

Lies / Truth

A truth that's told with bad intent
beats all the lies you can invent.
Blake

Doctors / Lawyers

Fond of doctors, little health. Fond of lawyers, little wealth.

Humor / Tragedy

It's humor when you fall in love.
It's tragedy when you fall out of love.

Education

It is better to be able neither to read
or write than to be able to do nothing else.
Hazlitt

College

You can lead a boy to college,
but you cannot make him think.
Elbert Hubbard

Judge Roy Bean

Judge Roy Bean divorced people he had married
(with no legal right to do so) saying he only aimed
to rectify his errors.

Idleness

Idleness is the stupidity of the body,
and stupidity is the idleness of the mind.
Seneca

Law

Probably all laws are useless; for good men do not need
laws at all, and bad men are made no better by them.
Demonah the Cynic

Success

Finding your own truths, developing your own
beliefs that are not favored.

Imagination

The lunatic, the lover, and the poet
are of imagination all compact.
Shakespeare

Aristocracy

Aristocracy is always cruel.

Cynic

A cynic knows the price of everything
and the value of nothing.
Oscar Wilde

CEO Income

In 1999 the average CEO of a major corporation made $12.4 million.

Knowledge

Knowledge is proud that he has learned so much;
Wisdom is humble that he knows no more.
Cowper

Great Satisfaction

There is great satisfaction in doing what others
say you cannot do.

Ignorance

Innocence plays in the back yard of ignorance.

Auto Repair

Seventy percent of major car repairs are the result of a lack
of maintaining vital fluids and maintenance.

Public Education

It is better to know worthless
information than to know nothing.

Anger

Flying into a rage makes for bad landings.

Honesty

A shady business never yields a sunny life.
B.C. Forbes

Hope
Patience is the art of hoping.
Vauvenargues

Humility
Nothing is so strong as gentleness,
nothing so gentle as real strength.
St. Francis de Sales

Idealism
We are an idealistic people and we'll make
any sacrifice for a cause that won't hurt business.

Fear
All is to be feared where all is to be lost.
Byron

Fidelity
When my love swears that she is made of truth,
I do believe her, though I know she lies.
Shakespeare

Love
There is no remedy for love but to love more.
Thoreau

Fools
I love fools experiments. I am always making them.
Darrwin

Courage

There is only one thing that requires real
courage to say, and that is a truism.
Gilbert Chesteston

Flattery

Flattery never comes up to the expectation of conceit.

Old Age Blessing

One of the blessings of old age is that you
no longer suffer from young age.

Fame

Fame is but the breath of the people,
and that often unwholesome.

Position For Women

The only position for women in SNCC is prone.
Stokely Carmichael

Eyes

I have a good eye, uncle; I can see a church by daylight.
Shakespeare

Facts

There are men who can think no deeper than a fact.
Voltaire

Epitaphs

Beneath this stone my wife doth lie;
now she's at rest, and so am I.

Government
The illegal we do immediately,
the unconstitutional takes a little longer.
Henry Kissinger

Fame
Nothing is more annoying than a low
man raised to a high position.
Claudian

Extravagance
A princely mind will undo a private family.
Lord Habifox

Money
Sudden money is going from zero to
two hundred dollars a week, the rest doesn't count.
Neil Simon

Epigrams
No epigram contains the whole truth.
C.W. Thompson

Love
Love comes unseen, we only see it go.
Austin Dobson

Danger
Always the danger of too much or too little.

Wild Oats

Wild oats will get sown some time, and one of the
arts of life is to sow them at the right time.
Richard Le Galbenne

Flirts

True love is the just dessert and cure for a flirt.

Chasing

Men chase women till they catch him.

Progress

Technological progress has merely provided
us with more efficient means for going backwards.
Aldous Huxley

Too Cultured

If you can't enjoy eating with your fingers,
you are too cultured.

Experience

I had six honest serving men,
they taught me all I know. Their names were:
where, what, when, why, how and who.
Kipling

Skill

Skill comes from intention and much experience.

Courtesy

A gentleman "invariably" follows a lady upstairs.

1973

The memominee retortions act reinstates
the Indian tribes trust status.

Police

The police are fully able to meet
and compete with all criminals.
Mayor Hylan

Weather

The weather on the first of the month is the
opposite of what the rest of the month will be.

Husbands

Her husband is an accountant but he can't figure her out.

Criminal

A criminal is a person with predatory instincts who
has not sufficient capital to form a corporation.
Howard Scott

Philosopher

A philosopher knows what to do until it happens to him.

Having

A thing worth having is a thing worth cheating for.
W.C. Fields

Deception

We are never deceived; we deceive ourselves.
Goethe

Doubt

Doubt motivates our education.

Proverbs

A proverb is a short sentence based on long experience.
Cervantes

Love

To love oneself is the beginning of a lifelong romance.
Oscar Wilde

Strong man

A strong man is giving not getting.

Good / Bad

When I'm good, I'm very good.
But when I'm bad, I'm better.
Mae West

Dying

More people die of old age than of young age.

Quiet

Quiet as the whisper of leaves on a calm day.

Illusion

Illusion is the first of all pleasures.
Voltaire

Understanding

I never understand anything until I have written about it.
Voltaire

President James Garfield

Garfield could write in Greek with one hand
and in Latin with the other at the same time.

Conscience

A guilty conscience is the mother of invention.
Carolyn Wells

Wrong Number

Well, if I called the wrong number,
why did you answer the phone?
James Thurber

Majority

Hain't we got all the fools in town on our side,
and ain't that a big enough majority in any town?
Mark Twain

Beware

Beware of all enterprise that require new clothes.
Henry David Thoreau

Grounds For Divorce

A Maine man divorced his wife cause
she wore earplugs whenever his mother came to visit.

Luck

There is no one luckier than he who thinks himself so.
German Proverb

Difference

The difference between in-laws
and outlaws is that outlaws are wanted.

1975

AIM and FBI shoot out at Pine Ridge Reservation.
Two agents die. Leonard Peltier sentenced,
most believe unjustly.

Lost

Great I found my car keys. Now, where the hell is my car.

Retired Couple With Dog

We're staying together for the sake of the dog.

Retired Knowledge

Retired, know it all and have time to tell you.

Good

Be not simply good, be good for something.
Henry David Thoreau

The World Needs

The world needs more whittlers and less chiselers.

Mi Casa Sa Casa

My house is your house.
Please feel free to make payments.

Life & Death

I believe in life before death.

Love

To love and win is the best thing;
to love and lose, the next best.
William Thackeray

Champion TV Watchers

Women over age of fifty five.

Men

The more I see of men, the more I like dogs.
Madame de Stael

Religious

All religious are founded on the fear of the
many and the cleverness of the few.
Marie Henri Beyle

Women

Women are wiser than men because they
know less and understand more.
James Stephens

Hug A Farmer

Fed your kid today? Hug a Farmer.

2 Out Of 3 Ain't Bad

Filthy, stinking, and rich. 2 out of 3 ain't bad.

Her Favorite

Her favorite thing to make for dinner is reservations.

Nature

Study & experience nature with your
10,000 year old longing.

Life

The first forty years of life give us the text;
the next thirty supply the commentary.
Arthur Schopemhauer

Preachers

Preachers say, do a I say, not as I do.
John Selden

Vices

He lacked only a few vices to be perfect.
Marguise de Sevigne

Sailors

Being in a ship is being in jail,
with the chance of being drowned.
Samuel Johnson

Round N Round

Trapped in that revolving door of politics.

Trash

Japanese & Germans create about 2.4 pounds of trash a
day per capita, about half of Americans.

Science

Everything has a cause and
the cause of anything is everything.
W.J. Turner

One Liners

Dentist

A dentist at work in his vocation
always looks down in the mouth.
George Prentice

1978

Congress passes the America Indian Freedom of
Religion Act, stating that Indian religions are
protected by the first amendment.

Lord And Soul

O Lord, if there is a Lord, save my soul, if I have a soul.

Ignorance

Everybody is ignorant, only on different subjects.
Will Rogers

Santa Spells

Santa = Satan

Charlie Chaplin

In the end, everything is a gag.
Charlie Chaplin

Wellness

Those who treat disease make
more money than those who treat health.

Fools

The fool doth think he is wise,
but the wise man knows himself to be a fool.
Shakespeare

Sane

An asylum for the sane would be empty in America.
George Bernard Shaw

History

History is more or less bunk.
Henry Ford

Doctors

Doctors will have more lives to answer for
in the next world than even we generals.
Napoleon

Leaning

If you're not leaning on them they won't let you down.

Chivalry

Going about releasing beautiful maidens from
other men's castles, and taking them to your own castle.
Henry Nevinsou

Folly

When folly is bliss, it's ignorant to be otherwise.
Ethel Mumford

Plagiarism - Research

Plagiarism is when you take stuff from one writer,
but when your take it form many writers, it's research.
Wilson Migner

Children

Children are not glue for a bad marriage, they're dynamite.

Hard Life

Life is hard and the first hundred years are the hardest.

Preference

Most prefer an exciting vice to a dull virtue.

Fools

Seeing she could not make fools wise,
fortune has made them lucky.
Michael Montaigne

Love Work

Work is love made visible.
Kahlil Gibram

Corruption

The corruption of a society may be measured
by the number of its laws.
Tacitus

Easy Way

There are many ways to do something.
Why is the easiest way always wrong?

Value

Marilyn Monroe and Adolf Hitler shared
a deep sense of worthlessness.

Choice

Most of the people are oblivious to real choice.

City Life
Millions of people being lonesome together.
Henry David Thoreau

Man
Every man wants a woman to appeal to his better side,
his noble instincts and his higher nature -
and another woman to help him forget them.
Helen Rowland

Essential
The spirit is essential to live a whole life.

Superstition
No sooner had Jesus knocked over the dragon of
superstition than Paul boldly sit it on it legs
again in the name of Jesus.
George Bernard Shaw

Being
Being is more important that learning.

1980
Federal census shows 1,418,195 Indians.

Work Reward
The best reward can be not what you get from
your work but what you become from your work.

Mindlessness
Isn't there a religion where mindlessness is a status symbol?

Weirdness

Weirdness proves the creator had a big imagination.

Kick

Even with your head in the sand,
you can't miss a kick in the ass.
Anne Wilson Schaef

Love

Nothing kills love like an overdose of it.

Children Question

What are you going to be if the neighbors let you grow up.

Life

Life is a sexually transmitted disease.
Guy Bellamy

Last Supper

A piece of cheese, spring loaded, last supper, never finished.

Time Lost

Time lost in anger, is time lost being joyful.

Opportunity Abundance

A mosquito in a nudist colony.

Relationships

When we let go of what relationships should be
and let relationships be what is, we have a chance
for relationships to be what they can be.
Anne Wilson Schaef

Seeing

I saw the most outrageous human this morning,
when I looked in the mirror.

Fanatic

A fanatic is one who can't change his mind
and won't change the subject.
Winston Churchill

Lighten Up

Lightening up never hurt anybody.

Work

Your work is to discover your work
and then with all your heart to give yourself to it.
Buddha

Speeches

Three things matter in a speech; who says it,
how he says it, and what he says, and, of the three,
the last matters the least.
John Morley

Diamond

I know I'm a diamond in the rough.

Truth And Love

The world is too dangerous for anything but truth
and too small for anything but love.

Codependent Heaven

The self-help section of a bookstore.

Thinking

An Englishman thinks seated; A Frenchman, standing; An American pacing; An Irishman, afterwards.
Austin O'Malley

Reality

Reality can ruin dreams.

Annoyance

Few things are harder to put up with than a good example.
Mark Twain

Straw Vote

A straw vote only shows which way the hot air blows.
O. Henry

Wise Mother

A wise mother remembers what a silly girl she was.

Dime Use

About the only use for a dime today is as a screwdriver.

Education

Six year old - Did you see the condom on the patio?
Other six year old - What's a patio?

Nostalgia

The fun of remembering with rearranging.

Fear

Fear can keep a man out of danger,
but courage only can support him in danger.

Hate
Never hate anyone as much as you think you should.

1990
Congress approves the Native American
Graves Protection and Repatriation Act.

Live
Live one day at a time, today only.

Vulgarity
Vulgarity is simply the conduct of others.
Oscar Wilde

Pessimist Noise
A pessimist complains about the
noise of opportunity knocking.

Hesitation
Those who hesitate are usually glad they did.

Can / Can't
Think you can, think you can't,
and either way you will be correct.
Henry Ford

Views
The man who views the world at fifty the same as
he did at twenty has wasted thirty years of his life.
Muhammad Ali

Seeing
Glasses don't help when your eyes are closed.

Talk
Talk is not cheap
and money talks

Truth
Believe those who seek the truth; doubt those who have found it.

Who's In Charge
A caterpillar is not in charge of becoming a butterfly.

Love
Being deeply loved by someone gives you strength,
while loving someone deeply gives you courage.

Normal
Sick is normal but it ain't normal.

God Contradiction
Many who say they don't believe in God
act like they are God.

Milk Addict
A milk addict is a cow-dependent.

Lying
There are better uses for your creativity than lying.

Problem Solving
Identifying the problem doesn't solve it but it's
hard to solve a problem without identifying it.

Young Women / Older Men
More young women interested in
older men 40-50 than 60-70.

Dying
When childhood dies, its corpses are called adults.
Brian Aldiss

Time
Time is a better healer than beautician.

Repeating History
History keeps repeating itself and the price keeps going up.

Pure Truth
Only the wilderness is pure truth.
Tom Brown Jr.

Men's Trouble
The trouble with men is their trouble with women.

Womans Vacation Choice
Go to the mountains and see the scenery or
go to the beach and be the scenery.

English Meaning
A fat chance and a slim chance are the same thing.

For Better Or For Worse
For better or for worse means that the groom
couldn't do better and the bride couldn't do worse.

Poets
Poets learn that rhyme doesn't pay.

Golden Rule
The golden rule is that there are no golden rules.
George Bernard Shaw

Insurance
The big print giveth and the small print taketh away.

Joke Test
If your wife laughs at your joke,
it means you have a good joke or a good wife.

Knowledge
All I know is what I read in the books I write.

Cauliflower
Cauliflower is nothing but cabbage
with a college education.
Mark Twain

Laws
Over a million laws to enforce the Ten Commandments.

Interstates

The Eisenhower interstate system requires that one mile is every five must be straight. The reason: the straight sections can be used as airstrips in war or emergencies.

Footprints

Footprints in the road of time aren't made sitting down.

1991

Federal Census shows almost 2 million Indians. Canadian Indians number 1,002,675.

Important Statistic

There are almost twice as many feet in the world as there are people.

Greatest Lesson

The greatest lesson in life is to know that even fools are right sometimes.

Men

Give a man a free hand and he'll run it all over you.
Mae West

Good Life

Life is as good as your heart is awake and alive.

Shortest Sentence

"I am." is the shortest complete sentence in the English language.

U.S. Presidents
No president was an only child.

Everything
Love, Share & Respect.

Womans Face
A woman's face may be her fortune,
but the other parts draw interest.

Success Is Relative
Success is relative. The more success, the more relatives.

Cooking Rice
The best way to keep rice from sticking
together is to boil each grain separately.

Gambling
Gambling away the rent money is a moving experience.

Main Difference Between A Rancher and A Politician
The main difference between a rancher and a politician is
that with a rancher the shit is on the outside of the boots.

Cows / Rain
Cows lying in the pasture indicate rain coming.

Church Slogan
The minister announced the tithing slogan last Sunday:
I upped my pledge - up yours.

Spiders
The average human eats 8 spiders
in their lifetime while sleeping.

Cockroaches
A cockroach can live 9 days without its
head before starving to death.

Aging
You're never too old to become younger.
Mae West

Elvis
Elvis had a twin brother named Aaron,
who died at birth, that's why Elvis' middle name
is Aaron, in honor of his brother.

Marilyn Monroe
Marilyn had six toes.

Dueling
Dueling is legal in Paragway as long as
both parties are registered blood donors.

Airplanes / Donkeys
More people are killed annually
by donkeys than in plane crashes.

Stewardesses
Stewardesses is the longest word
typed with only the left hand.

Truth

Some what dangerous, but beautiful and precious.

Church Bulletin

We invite any member of the congregation
who enjoys sinning to join the choir.

Success

Only in the dictionary does success come before work.

Geronimo de Mendieta

A distinguished Francsian monk and historian stated that
the massive Indian die-off was God's punishment to the
Spanish for their horrendous mistreatment of the Indians.

Catholic Split

The Catholic church has split into 2 separate organizations,
one is the high mass and the other is the low mass.

Chocolate

The average chocolate bar has 8 insect legs in it.

College Major

He majored in extra curricular activities.

Cash Future

We can only accept cash with proper identification.

Heaven and Hell

The same kind of people go to
heaven as go to hell, dead ones.

Divorce
Only in the dictionary does divorce come before marriage.

White America Cultural Denial
The book "American Holocaust" cuts thru the denial into
the core of European thinking, culture, Christianity,
sex, racism and violence.

Motives
Whenever a man does a thoroughly stupid thing,
it is always from the noblest motives.
Oscar Wilde

Learning
One pound of learning requires ten
pounds of common sense to apply it.

Children
Each family should have three children,
if one is a genius, the other two can support him.

Love And Time
Love makes time pass, and time makes love pass.

Women's Fashions
It's fashionable for women to wear mens clothes, up to a
point, even women are smart enough not to wear neckties.

Happiness
Happiness can always be found in the dictionary.

Christmas Super Bargain

Christmas trees right after Christmas.

Milk Cows

No matter what color the cow is the milk is white.

Love

A man in love sees a pimple as a dimple.
Japanese Proverb

Vegetarian Beef

We guarantee that our cattle have never eaten meat.

Advice

Advice and prescription come from others,
solutions are our actions.

Columbus

The embodiment and result of over a thousand years
of Christian, European culture. A religious fanatic
obsessed with conversion, conquest, extermination
of all non-Christians. A glory hound seeking
personal power, wealth and fame.

Be Courageous

Courage is pretending to be brave when you're not.

Judge Roy Bean

Judge Roy Bean freed an Irishman who had killed a
Chinaman, saying there was no law in his book
against killing a Chinaman.

Justice 1998

A San Antonio man was jailed for possession of methamphetamine. Unable to make bail he lost his job, pickup, apartment and military reserve status.
The police field test showed the presence of the drug. He claimed this substance to be the ashes of his grandmother. A later test confirmed the substance was human remains.

Stress Relief

For stress relief, laugh at inappropriate times.

Children

Children begin by loving their parents; as they grow older they judge them; sometimes they forgive them.
Oscar Wilde

Love

Love sought is good, but given unsought is better.
Shakespeare

Mistakes

Wise men learn by other men's mistakes,
fools by their own.

Doctor Translations

I'd like to have my associate look at you,
translates to, he owes me some money.

Learning

The only things worth learning are
the things you learn after you know it all.
Harry Truman

Failure / Success

No good thing is failure and no evil thing is success

Male And Female

Male and female are really two cultures
and their experiences are utterly different.
Kate Millett

Wilderness

For the Lakota there was no wilderness... nature was not
dangerous but susceptible, not forbidding but friendly.

Facts

Facts stab us in the back.

Las Vegas

Our neighbor flew his own airplane to Las Vegas
to get away from it all. They got it all away
from him - including his plane.

Men

Men are beasts, and even beasts don't behave as they do.
Brigitte Bardot

Wisdom

Still waters run deep.

Man / God

Man proposes, God disposes.

People Test

Traveling with someone is the best people test.

Learning

I hear and I forget. I see and I remember.
I do and I understand.
Chinese proverb

Love

A man loved by a beautiful woman
will always get out of trouble.
Voltaire

Truth

As scarce as truth is, the supply
has always been in excess of the demand.
Josh Billings

Fate

Hanging and winning goes by destiny.
Shakespeare

Christs Teachings

The only people on Earth who do not see Christ & his
teaching as non-violent are Christians.
Gandi

Eternity

Eternity is right now.

Virtues

To be good is noble, but to teach others
to be good is even nobler, and less trouble.
Mark Twain

Education
All education is self education.

Birds
Many hear the birds sing, few hear their joy.

Homeless USA 1998
400,000 plus families 1.2 million children homeless.
The average homeless persons age is 9.

Humility
The most difficult aspect of humility
is that you can't brag about it.

Temptations
These are several good protections against temptation,
but the surest is cowardice.
Mark Twain

Wounds
All soldiers of war are wounded.

Teaching
You cannot teach a man anything;
you can only help him find it within himself.
Galileo

This
This too shall pass.

Wise Man

A wise man sees as much as he ought,
not as much as he can.
Montaigne

Living

Live and let live.

Traveling Companion

Easier to find a traveling companion than to get rid of one.

Observation

You can observe a lot by just watching.
Yogi Bera

Philosophers

There is no record in human history of a happy philosopher.
H.L. Mencken

The Six Phases Of Project Development

1. Wild enthusiasm 2. Disillusionment. 3. Total confusion.
4. Search for the guilty. 5. Punishment of the innocent.
6. Promotion of nonparticipants.

Failure Plans

Most people don't plan to fail, they fail to plan.

Time

Time heals and then it kills.

Letters
Write thank you letters in a timely fashion.

Errors
To err is human, but it feels divine.
Mae West

Politics
The more you read about politics, the more you
got to admit that each party is worse than the other.
Will Rogers

Life
Life ain't your moment of embodiment.

Native America Criminal Class
There is no distinctly Native
American criminal class except congress.
Mark Twain

Procrastinators Never Die
Old procrastinators never die, they just keep putting it off.

Give
Give unexpected gifts

Recreation
When a man wantonly destroys one of the works of
man we call him a vandal. When he wantonly destroys
one of the works of God we call him a sportsman.
Joseph Wood Kurtch

Angels

We wake up as angels, become demons,
go to sleep and become angels again.

Talking

Don't talk to me when I'm interrupting.
Sam Goldwyn

Talking

Wise men talk because they have something to say;
fools talk because they have to say something.
Plato

Letter Of Recommendation

I encourage you to waste no time in
making this person an offer of employment.

Time

Right now in this moment is time.

Study

Anything studied long enough becomes more complex.

Names

Dr. Zolten Ovary is a Gynecologist.

Consistency

Consistency is the last refuge of the unimaginative.
Oscar Wilde

Cooperation

Coming together is a beginning; keeping together is progress, working together is success.
Henry Ford

Courage

It takes as much courage to try &
fail as it does to try & succeed.

New Systems

New systems generate new problems.

Men

I only like two kinds of men - domestic and foreign.
Mae West

First Law Of Systems Planning

Anything that can be changed will
be changed until there is no time left to change anything.

Aging

I think aging is a nightmare.
Sylvester Stallone

Humility

One may be humble out of pride.
Montaigne

Life

It's a funny old world,
a man's lucky if he can get out of it alive.
W.C. Fields

Virtue

Don't be misled into the paths of virtue.
Oscar Wilde

Funerals

There is no point going to someone's funeral
as you know they won't be coming to yours.

Consistency

The only completely consistent people are the dead.
Aldous Huxley

Social Change

Technology is the most subtle and the most effective
engineer of enduring social change. Its apparent
neutrabilty is deceptive and often disarming.
Robert MacIver

Measure

When alive we measure by their worst,
when dead we measure by their best.

Failure

Any man who has $10,000 left when he dies is a failure.
Errol Flynn

Religion In 1998

The president of the National Baptist Convention
USA was charged with 56 counts of fraud, extortion,
money laundering, conspiracy and tax evasion.
He faces a maximum 815 years in prison
and $25 million in fines.

Idealism

An idealist is a person who helps
other people to be prosperous.
Henry Ford

Decisions

Nothing will ever be attempted if all
possible objections must be overcome first.

Education

The education of a man is never completed until he dies.
Robert E. Lee

Flowing Communications

Flowing communicatios don't flow,
they leak, spurt and dribble.

Your Life Is

Your life is experiencing & learning. Go for it!

Theory

A little experience upsets a lot of theory.
S. Parkes Cadman

Words

A word of encouragement during a failure is worth more
than a whole book of praise after a success.

Facts

There are no facts, only interpretations.
Friedrich Mietzsche

Understanding

Will you even begin to understand the meaning of the
very soil beneath your feet? From a grain of sand to
a great mountain, all is sacred. Yesterday and
tomorrow exist eternally upon this continent.
We are natures' guardians of this sacred place.
Peter Blue Cloud - Mohawk

Reasons

A person always has two reasons for
doing anything, a good reason and the real reason.
J. Pierpont Morgan

Details

Don't be more precise than the subject warrants.
Plato

Circumstances

Your circumstances reflect what you believe.

Failure

Every mans got to figure to get beat sometimes.
Joe Louis

Optimists / Pessimist

The man who is a pessimist before forty-eight
knows too much; the man who is an optimist after
forty-eight knows too little.
Mark Twain

Women

Woman begins by resisting a man's advances
and ends by blocking his retreats.
Oscar Wilde

Beware

Beware the man who won't be bothered with details.

Hottest Reservations

The hottest places in hell are reserved for those who, in
times of great moral crises, maintain their neutrality.
Dante

Quiet

Quiet as a thief in a chicken house.

Failure

Everyone except a skydiver is
allowed an occasional failure.

World Condition Of People

There is something wrong when two-thirds of the people
are starving and one-third are dieting.

Premature Graves

Premature graves are mostly dug with the mouth.

Failure

Failure is only the opportunity to
begin again more intelligently.
Henry Ford

Respect / Love

Respect is what we owe; love is what we give.
Philip Bailey

Economics

Blessed are the young,
for they shall inherit the national debt.
Herbert Hoover

Glory

Our greatest glory is not in never failing,
but in rising everytime we fail.
Confucius

Price

All good things are cheap; all bad are very dear.
Thoreau

Food / Population

Intensification of production to feed an increased
population leads to a still greater increase in population.
Peter Farb

Medium Of Exchange

Let's change the medium of exchange from money to love.

Speeches

When words are scarce they are seldom spent in vain.
Shakespeare

Pride

There is this paradox in pride, it makes some men ridiculous, but prevents other from becoming so.
C.C. Colton

Faults

The greatest of faults is to be conscious of none.
Thomas Carlyle

Foolish

If fifty million people say a foolish thing,
it is still a foolish thing.
Anatole Franse

Remember

Remember that you are part of the people who can be fooled some of the time.

Friends

The meeting of two personalities is like the contact of two chemical substances: if there is any reaction, both are transformed.
C. G. Jung

Future

The past is but the beginning of a beginning and all that is and has been is but the twilight of the dawn.
H. G. Wells

Importance

On reflection I often couldn't tell, at the time, whether an action was important.

Happiness

Neither poverty or wealth can bring happiness.

God

If God lived on Earth, people would break his windows.
Yiddish Proverb

Habits

Form good habits, they're as hard to break as bad ones.

Wise Behavior

People behave wisely after being severely
burned by all the other choices.

Relaxation

Relaxation is taking the time to appreciate.

History

Not even God can not change the past,
however historians can and do.

Honesty

People are more shocked by honesty
and truth than by lies and illusions.

People

People are divided into two groups, the righteous
and the unrighteous, and the righteous do the dividing.

Genius

Geniuses always come with some madness.

Cost Of Living
In spite of the high cost, living is still popular.

Doing
Man who say it cannot be done
should not interrupt man doing it.
Chinese proverb

Best Humor
The best humor makes you laugh first and think second.

Arizona Progress
Before it was dammed up the Colorado River's main
channel often shifted. One morning an Arizonan who lived
on the bank of the river went out to inspect the damage from
an overnight flood and discovered that the river had made
a new channel on the other side of the house. He went
in and told his wife "Well, dear we live in California now."
She replied "Oh, thank God, I couldn't stand another
summer in Arizona."

Ideas
Ideas are like grandchildren, yours are the best.

Leadership
Lead, follow, or get out of the way.
Ted Turner

Purpose
Everyone has a useful purpose in life,
if nothing else but to be a bad example.

Funds

All my available funds are completely tied up in ready cash.
W.C. Fields

Good / Bad

I am as bad as the worst but, thank God,
I am as good as the best.
Walt Whitman

Kindness

You can never do a kindness too soon
because you never know how soon it will be two late.
Ralph Waldo Emerson

Living

Begin at once to live, and count each day as a seperate life.
Seneca

Trouble

You can get in trouble by being right at the wrong time.

Faith

All the darkness in the world
can't put out the light of one candle.
Confucius

Fools Gold

Miners find gold where it should be,
fools find gold where it is.

Dogma

Every dogma must have its day.
Carolyn Wells

President William Howard Taft

Taft was the only president to get struck in the
white house bathtub, requiring his aids to help get out.

Charity

Charity creates a multitude of sins.
Oscar Wilde

Civilization

Civilization takes time and time is running out.

Adam

Adam was human, he didn't want the apple for the apples
sake, he wanted it because it was forbidden.
Mark Twain

Love Poet

At the touch of love, everyone becomes a poet.
Plato

Women

Wicked women bother one; good women bore one;
that is the only difference between them.
Oscar Wilde

Luck

If your ship doesn't come in, swim out to it.
Jonathan Winters

Loss / Gain

Something lost, something gained;
something gained, something lost.

Possessions

Better ain't more possessions.

Organization Management

In any organization, there is someone who really
knows what's going on, that person must be fired.

Mature / Immature

An immature man wants to die nobly for a cause,
a mature man wants to live humbly for one.
Wilkelm Stekel

Cost

Sometimes one pays most for the things
one gets for nothing.
Albert Einstein

Money

Money can't buy independence.

Possibilities

There are always other possibilities.

Anger

When you're angry at someone pray
for them until you can respond with love.

Unhappy

Unhappy wanting it, unhappy getting it,
unhappy in fear of losing it.

Morals
Cowards can never be moral.
Gandhi

Optimist / Pessimist
The optimist is as wrong as the pessimist, only happier.

Decisions
The best time to make a decision is
before your have to make one.

Character And Reputation
Character is made of what you stood for;
reputation by what you fall for.

Love
To a woman in love, loving too much is not loving enough.

Failure
A failure is a man who has blundered but is
not able to cash in the experience.
Elbert Hubbard

The Church
The church must be reminded that it is not the master or the
servant of the state, but rather the conscience of the state.
Martin Luther King, Jr.

Meeting Gratitude
First, I want to thank the people
who made this meeting necessary.
Yogi Bera

Children Needs

Children need more models and less critics.

Life

Life wanders. It stops to explore.
It falls down and gets up and brushes itself off.
That Avatar understands this is one of its strengths.
Harry Palmer

Committees

Committees: never has so little been done by so many.

Expertise

His expertise was in his own ignorance.

Communication Importance

The most important thing to hear
anyone saying is what isn't being said.

Powerful Drug

Words are the most powerful drug used by mankind.
Rudyard Kipling

Wisdom

Wise men learn from other's mistakes, fools by their own.

Truth

Every truth passes through three stages before it is
recognized. In the first it is ridiculed, in the second it is
opposed, and in the third it is regarded as self evident.
Arthur Schopenhauer

Names

Every Tom, Dick and Harry is named William.
Sam Goldwyn

Foolin A Man

For a woman, foolin a man is easy;
what's hard is findin one that's not a fool.

Smart

To a smart girl men are no problem they're the answer.
Zsa Zsa Gabor

Idleness

It is better to play than do nothing.
Confucius

Humility

Be humble or you'll stumble.
Dwight Moody

Love

He who tries to forget a woman has never loved her.

Patriotism

Patriotism is a kind of religion;
it is the egg from which wars are hatched.
Gay de Maupossant

Aging

One who sees never grows old.

Perseverance

A man in earnest finds means,
or if he cannot find, creates them.
Channing, William

Man

Man is a two-legged animal without feathers.
Plato

Elizabeth Taylor

I've been through it all, baby I'm mother courage.
Elizabeth Taylor

Blackjack

When playing blackjack,
assume that unseen cards are an eight.

Life

All life is interdependent.

Women & Money

If women didn't exist, all the money
in the world would have no meaning.
Aristotle Onassis

Fear

They that worship God merely from fear,
would worship the devil too, if he appear.

Politicians

A politician - one that would circumvent God.
Shakespeare

Selfishness

Ultimately what is the best for me is the best for everyone
and everything.

Line Up

Now all you fellers line up alphabetically by height.
Casey Stengel

Religious

All the religions are narrow and limiting.

Vaccinations

Vaccines being cultured on animal organs has resulted in
animal to human transmission of viruses.

Word Of Honor

If you can't give me your word of honor,
will you give me your promise?
Samuel Goldwyn

Power

A friend in power is a friend lost.
Henry Adams

Praise

Compliments cost nothing, yet many pay dear for them.

Prayer

A good deed is the best prayer.
Robert Ingersoll

Healthy

We are healthy only to the extent that
our ideas are humane.
Kurt Vonnegut, Jr.

The Masses

The mass of men lead lives of quiet desperation.
Henry David Thoreau

Love and Marriage

Venus, a beautiful good-natured lady, was
the goddess of love; Juno, a terrible shrew, the goddess
of marriage; and they were always mortal enemies.
Jonathon Swift

Emotions

The advantage of the emotions is that they lead us astray.
Oscar Wilde

Oldest Joke

When Eve asked Adam:
Do you love me? and he replied, who else?

Knowledge

Everybody knows more than somebody,
but nobody knows more than everybody.

Originality

Originality is nothing but judicious imitiation.
Voltaire

Nite

Nite is day for sinners.

Preaching

He charged nothing for his preaching, and it was worth it, too.
Mark Twain

Christians

The last Christian died on the cross.
Fredrich Wilhelm

My Granddaughter

My granddaughter Timmari reported in her paper
that during the Civil war, Connecticut was very
valuable in producing arms and other body parts.

Wisdom

Knowledge comes but wisdom lingers.
Tennyson

Church Bulletin

The Rev. Smith spoke briefly,
much to the delight of the audience.

Big Deal

In 1997, in the biggest banking deal in US history,
First Union Corp. announced the purchase of
Core States Financial Corp. for $16.1 billion.

Amazing Solutions

Several people sharing their ignorance
can often come up with solutions.

Politics and Ageism

1998: John Glenn at 77 went back out into space in glory.
1997: Story Musgrave after 30 years in the space program
was told at age 61 that he would never fly again.

Beautiful Flowers

Admiring, smelling beautiful flowers, weddings & funerals,
in the garden, in the yard, and everywhere;
people giving so much attention to the sexual organs of
plants while hiding their own.

Swag

Swag is a scientific term used throughout science,
engineering & construction of all kinds.
S= Scientific   W=Wild   A=Ass   G=Guess

Nature

Study, learn & honor the real laws of nature (God).

Live Simply

Live simply, so others may simply live.

Shifts

Shifts happen.

Namaste

I honor the place within you where the entire universe
resides. I honor the place within you of love and light,
of peace & truth. I honor the place within you where,
when you are in that place in you and I am in
that place in me, thre is only one of us.
Namaste

Criticism
All criticism is self criticism.

The Light
Unconditional love is the light.

Freedom
Freedom is not given, it is created.

Everything
Everything is part of you.

AA
AA Amusement & amazement.

Struggle
To end struggle, quit struggling.

Teaching Advice
After teaching, step aside.

Societies Success
The difference in the treatment of the best & worst members of a society is the measure of that societies success.

Identity
Be who you really are.

Reality
Love & light cannot be replaced with darkness.

Life
See the golden threads, see the golden web of all life.

Change
Change your feelings by changing your beliefs.

Your Behavior
We are all children and are following you and your example.

Today, Tomorrow & Forever
What is the short term solution?
What is the long term solution?

Better Life
Better is the highest expression of yourself.

Stuff, Forget It
Forget about acquiring all that "Stuff" instead
focus on your experience & truth of your spiritual being.

Money In The USA
Top one percent have more than the bottom ninety percent.

Delivery Service
Become a Spiritual Warrior delivering love,
healing & celebration.

Common Illusions
The illusions of superiority & seperateness.

Nebraska's Biggest Holiday

Nebraska's biggest holiday is the annual
day of Swine & Roses.

Inspiration

With inspiration, miracles happen.

Current Change Happening

We are changing from materialism to spiritualism.

Winners? Losers?

In the game of romance, sometimes the winners are the
losers and the losers are the winners.

Soda Pop

Consumption of soda pop in the USA per capita is
100 gallons a year per person.

Mosquito Bites

The purpose of mosquito bites are to remind
us that we are part of the food change.

Common Cold Prevention Study

Researchers at Wilkes University in Pa. Discovered higher
levels of a cold fighting antibody in people who
have sex one or more times a week than
those who have sex less frequently.

Best Two Gifts For Children

Give children roots & give them wings.

Indian Artist

I won't paint pretty pictures, I'm nobody's dancing bear.
Robert Penn - Lakota Artist

Manhood

Manhood ain't conquest!!! Try cooperation & consent.

Lent

He always gave up his New Year's resolutions for lent.

Progress In America

It ain't easy to be an American Indian in America.

Nature

Nature doesn't pay any attention to the color of people's skin.

Real Men

Real men never quit!

Cadillac Casket

Rich Texan buried in his Cadillac, let it rust in peace.

Happiness

Pursuing, possessing or protecting any "thing" to make you
happy doesn't work…Seek happiness where you lost it.
Harry Palmer

Cleaning Copper

Cut a lemon, dip in salt and rub on
copper to clean and brighten.

Nebraska / Wyoming Wind

The wind blows so hard from Wyoming
because Nebraska sucks.

Culture Takes Time

Culture takes time, so much culture, so little time.

War Preparation

Boyscouts & Sports prepare boys for war.

Hope

The hope of future generations is the chance we have to
awaken in ourselves a consciousness that is increasingly
immune to irrationality and that values wisdom.
The world has been waiting a very long time
for the appearance of wisdom.
Harry Palmer

Here Now

I am here now, with you, me and everything.

Agreements

Honor you agreements.

Freedom

Your freedom ends where mine begins.

Great Plains View

Some of us look out across the plains and see
Buffalo forever in all directions.

Heartland Publishing
JOEL RANDALL
WRITER: ESSAYS & POEMS of the Heartland - programs available.
COLLECTOR: TRUCKS, PICKUPS & CARS 1935-1965

Order Form

Books

ONE LINERS
by Joel Randall   _____ @ 19.95 each   _____

REFLECTION & PERCEPTIONS
by Joel Randall   _____ @ $14.95 each   _____

COWBOY OR FARMER?
by Joel Randall   _____ @ $9.95 each   _____

ESSENCE
by Joel Randall   _____ @ $9.95 each   _____

Audio Cassette Tapes

FARM AND RANCH MEMORIES
by Joel Randall   _____ @ $7.00 each   _____

Shipping & Handling $3.00   _____

Total Enclosed   _____

Please send your order to:
Joel Randall
Heartland Publishing
P.O. Box 402
Seymour, MO 65746
(417) 935-9146

Entertaining programs are available for any occasion.

One Liners _____

TEAR OUT
THIS PAGE
AND
ORDER THAT GIFT
FOR
SOMEONE SPECIAL.

Index

C

I

J

O

One Liners

One Liners_____

One Liners_____

One Liners

Y

Z

Readers Notes

ABOUT THE AUTHOR
Joel Randall 1939-?

Grew up northwest of Gibbon, Nebraska with crops and livestock. Attended a one room school, graduated from college in Kearney, Corporate educated in finance, insurance and soda pop, while living in Scottsdale, Arizona.

Part of a "Summerhill" type school in New Mexico. Built a place, trained horses, milked goats, fed the hogs. Established a plumbing business. Developed an alternative healing center. Owned and operated a motel and mobile home business. Home in the Ozarks and on the family farm/ranch in Nebraska. Head out with the RV and home is wherever I park it. Life is full, with lots of friends and family. Interests include: writing, reading, rockabilly music, health and healing, real history, culture, tribalism, community, conscousness and enlightment.

Published: Auto Clubs & Writers Groups Newsletters, This Old Truck, Dry Creek Review, Twelve Steps Times, Mile High Poetry Society Anthology "Helicon", Santa Fe Sun, Santa Fe Reporter, Man Alive, Mother Earth News, Self published books and audio cassettes.

Readings & Programs: Schools, Retirement facilities, Coffee houses, Cowboy poetry gatherings, Literature festivals, and storytelling gatherings. Various celebrations and events in Arizona, Colorado, Nebraska, Nevada, New Mexico, Kansas, Missouri and Texas.

Bookings: programs custom tailored to your needs. Educational, entertaining and humorous topics presented to support your objectives. Contact: Joel Randall at 417-935-9146, joel_o_randall@hotmail.com or sarvis2joel@yahoo.com.

Website www.frontier.net/heartland